Endorsements on Behalf of

Resilient Leaders

Today's Marines and their families, as well as members of our other Armed Services, need all the help we can give them. General Dees' *Resilient Warriors* has been an urgently needed contribution to their personal resilience. Now this Outstanding Military Commander and business leader brings us his personal experiences through *Resilient Leaders*, for all ages and levels of responsibility, basically a guide for the leaders of today by providing them the tools and examples to help navigate the challenges that every leader faces.

H. Gene Overstreet
12th Sergeant Major of the United States Marine Corps
President and National Commander of the
Non Commissioned Officer Assn.
President and CEO of Leatherneck.com
President of Veterans Direct
Co-Chairman of the Marine Corps and Navy Retiree Council
Former Chairman for the Texas Veterans Coalition

***

It's been said, "The worth of one's character is measured by the trial of adversity." *Resilient Leaders* is a clear, compelling, and a full of common sense guide to handling and even thriving in adversity. Leaders not only need to be resilient, but they need to model resiliency to inspire those they lead. Life is a test and this book will help you be a good test taker!

I've known Bob Dees since Cadet days at West Point... He's the real deal and gets an A+ on the resiliency test.

Robert L. VanAntwerp
Lieutenant General, U.S. Army, Retired

***

I have known General Bob Dees for almost twenty years and have found him to be a man of vision, clarity, and principle. He has the capacity to distill ideas related to both following Jesus and leading people like few others. The wealth of experience in the crucible of conflict that Bob brings to his writing does more than inform me. It challenges me to look farther, think more precisely, and act boldly. *Resilient Leaders* calls me to practical leadership and it should. Bob Dees models it.

Reverend Dick Foth
Minister, Church Planter, Speaker, Author

***

I read *Resilient Warriors* and couldn't wait to get my hands on *Resilient Leaders*. As the President and CEO of a financial services company, the years since 2008 have certainly tried all of my skills as a corporate leader. Not only were clients looking to me for direction, but my team needed the reassurance that everything was going to be okay.

In reading *Resilient Leaders* I realized there were times when my twenty-five years of innate leadership paid off. But it also identified areas of weakness I wish I had known how to handle. Unfortunately in life we don't get "do overs," so we have to learn from both our mistakes and others' wisdom. I can say I am glad I have the wisdom of General Dees from which to draw.

Resilient Leaders is a book that should be read and re-read by everyone from parents to MBA students to CEO's of America. No one on the planet is more tried and tested than a General in today's Army. Kudos to General Dees for his ability to articulate concepts with universal application.

Erin Botsford
President and CEO, The Botsford Group

***

As a seasoned leader, General Bob Dees has captured the essence of resiliency in a leader. Leadership is always played out in the "Red Zone," and leaders who do not cultivate resiliency find themselves sidelined much too quickly. *Resilient Leaders* is a "must read" for anyone in a leadership role.

Dr. Andrew B. Seidel
Executive Director
Howard G. Hendricks Center for Christian Leadership
Dallas Theological Seminary

***

Resilient Leaders

The Resilience Trilogy

Major General Bob Dees
US Army, Retired

www.ResilienceTrilogy.com

Creative Team Publishing
San Diego

SCRIPTURE REFERENCES:
All scripture quotations, unless otherwise indicated, are taken from the New American Standard Bible, Copyright © 1960, 1962, 1963, 1968, 1971, 1972, 1973, 1975, 1977, 1995 by The Lockman Foundation. Used by permission. (http://www.Lockman.org)
Scripture quotations marked (NKJV) are taken from the New King James Version. NKJV™ Copyright © 1982 by Thomas Nelson, Inc. Used by permission. All rights reserved.
Scripture quotations marked (NIV) are taken from the Holy Bible, New International Version® NIV® Copyright © 1973, 1978, 1984, 2011 by Biblica, Inc.® Used by permission. All rights reserved worldwide.
Scripture quotations marked (NLT) are taken from the Holy Bible, New Living Translation, copyright © 1996, 2004, 2007. Used by permission of Tyndale House Publishers, Inc., Carol Stream, Illinois 60188. All rights reserved.

DISCLAIMERS:
This book is not a substitute for appropriate medical or psychological care for those experiencing significant emotional pain or whose ability to function at home, school, or work is impaired. Chronic or extreme stress may cause a wide assortment of physical and psychological problems. Some may require evaluation and treatment by medical or mental health professionals. When in doubt, seek advice from a professional.

You must not rely on the information in this book as an alternative to medical advice from your doctor or other professional healthcare provider. If you have any specific questions about any medical matter you should consult your doctor or other professional healthcare provider. If you think you may be suffering from any medical condition you should seek immediate medical attention. You should never delay seeking medical advice, disregard medical advice, or discontinue medical treatment because of information in this book.

During the process of constructing this book, due diligence has been undertaken to obtain all proper copyright permissions. If it comes to our attention that any citations are missing, they will be readily provided at http://www.ResilienceTrilogy.com.

See Permissions and Credits.

ISBN: 978-0-9855979-9-3
PUBLISHED BY CREATIVE TEAM PUBLISHING
www.CreativeTeamPublishing.com
San Diego
Printed in the United States of America

Resilient Leaders

The Resilience Trilogy

Major General Bob Dees

US Army, Retired

www.ResilienceTrilogy.com

Table of Contents

Foreword
Oliver L. North
Lieutenant Colonel
United States Marine Corps, Retired

If you haven't already read *Resilient Warriors* by my friend Major General Bob Dees, you should. It's a superb contribution for everyone who needs "bounce"—meaning all of us. *Resilient Warriors* is a work particularly valuable and relevant to our nation's veterans, those on active duty and the families of military personnel selflessly serving in some of the most difficult and dangerous places on earth. As I wrote in my endorsement:

> "America's heroes have been at war for more than a decade, selflessly defending our nation. They are the brightest and bravest of their generation. General Bob Dees knows the dangers they have faced, the sacrifices they have made, and

the challenges confronting their loved ones. If you know a veteran of a long ordeal, *Resilient Warriors* is a 'must read' for them—and for you."

Now we have another inspiring and equally relevant work by Bob Dees: *Resilient Leaders*.

Bob Dees knows leadership. He has been a selfless and resilient leader throughout his careers in the military, business, non-profit ministry to our nation's military and now as the leader of our nation's first Institute for Military Resilience at Liberty University. He has led through life and death situations, dire circumstances where everyone looked to him for guidance and hope. He has taken organizations in crisis and led them to higher ground, to new potential and productivity. Bob knows well the loneliness of a leader who shoulders the heavy load of responsibility for the welfare of many others. He has also experienced the highest reward of leadership: watching a team that has been carefully shaped and served as they accomplish things they never thought possible. Along the way, he has mastered the requisite qualities to mentor others in a vital life skill—leading others. In short, Bob Dees is a magnificent example of a truly Resilient Leader.

In this work, Bob asserts "leadership is a contact sport" and "leadership makes a difference." He's right. I have observed the essential truth of these axioms over many decades of leading and being led. I have seen great leaders and poor ones. Of this I am certain: good leadership makes all the difference in the world. Whether it's military service, national security affairs, business, politics, the media or in our communities and families—good leaders produce good outcomes. I'm convinced *Resilient Leaders* will make a difference in your life as a leader, helping you develop resilience in yourself, those you lead, and the organizations you influence.

For me, leadership has been one of the highest callings and most rewarding experiences of my life. I have also found that leadership can be tough, sometimes grueling, often requiring all the "bounce,"—resilience—I could muster. Since shortly after the terrible attacks of 9-11-01, Fox News has given me the privilege of covering brave young Americans on battlefields in downright inhospitable places around the globe.

While "embedded" with U.S. units in this long fight, I've had the opportunity to ask countless courageous young Soldiers, Sailors, Airmen, Guardsmen and Marines what prompted them to volunteer to serve our country in harm's way. Nearly all of them speak of role models who inspired them with grit, determination and the ability to rebound from adversity. In short, they are motivated by resilient leaders.

Though I'm now in my seventieth year, I still have such role models. Joe Reynolds immediately comes to mind.

"Daddy Joe," as many called him, had every opportunity to quit in life, yet, he managed to bounce back—seemingly higher than before—with every challenge. He enlisted in the Marines after Pearl Harbor in December 1941 and fought across the Pacific until he was seriously wounded during the vicious battle on Iwo Jima. Characteristic of Joe's tenacity and despite his wounds, he refused to be evacuated back to the states—and insisted on returning to the fight. He served as an artillery forward observer, calling in supporting fires for his fellow Marines until the battle for "Bloody Iwo" was won.

After World War II, Joe attended law school at Baylor University, where he was quickly recognized as a prodigy. After graduating with honors, Joe joined a prestigious Texas law firm and found himself in the forefront of several highly visible court cases. But on June 25, 1950, just as his promising law career was poised for takeoff, communist North Korea launched a surprise attack against their southern neighbor.

Within a week of the invasion, Joe was one of thousands of Marine officers recalled to active duty for service in the Korean War. For some—the prospect of having a lucrative new career derailed by another war would have been devastating. But not for this resilient leader.

Captain Joe Reynolds, USMC, reported for duty at Camp Pendleton, California, and on September 15, 1950, he was with the 1st Marine Division in a surprise amphibious assault behind enemy lines at Inchon, Korea. Joe's regimental commander, the legendary Lewis "Chesty" Puller, led Joe and his comrades through the liberation of South Korea's capital, Seoul, and then north toward the Chinese-North Korean border.

By November 27, Joe and his fellow Marines were at the Chosin Reservoir when they were surrounded and attacked by more than 100,000 Communist Chinese troops. For the next seventeen days, in temperatures reaching forty below zero, the 1st Marine Division broke out of the trap and fought its way to the

Korean coast. The epic battle took a horrific toll on the Americans. Joe and thousands of our troops suffered from wounds and frostbite during the brutal fight. Decades afterwards I met Joe at a gathering of the "Chosin Few"—the association of those who battled their way out of that terrible trap. I asked Joe for his most vivid memories of the breakout. He said, "Most of all I remember the bitter cold. That's why I decided to practice law in Houston, Texas. It just doesn't snow here!"

Though Joe spent months in the hospital recovering from battle wounds and severe frostbite, I never heard him complain once about the residual physical disabilities that he quietly endured for the rest of his life. After I filed a report on cases of Post Traumatic Stress (PTS) in Iraq, Joe called to tell me he had seen the story and acknowledged he too had suffered bouts of what he called "flashbacks" in which he would awaken at night, reliving the terrors of Iwo Jima and the Chosin Reservoir. I asked Joe if he ever received any treatment and he replied, "Oh yes, I learned to pray myself back to sleep."

Joe Reynolds' life experiences would have put many of us down for the count. Yet, he managed to bounce back. For him, obstacles were opportunities. He returned to the practice of law and became an extraordinary success—a leader in his church, his community, and profession. By employing the same character, courage, and competence that made him a successful Marine combat leader, he was recognized as a brilliant trial lawyer and voted a "Texas Legal Legend" by the Texas State Bar.

Perhaps most importantly, Joe Reynolds was a leader who demonstrated the remarkable power of being a positive role model. With Susie, his wife of 61 years at his side, Joe persevered through some of the toughest challenges anyone could have in life—to epitomize resilient leadership.

Resilient Leaders cuts right through the glamour of leadership to the heart of selfless service on behalf of others, to the critical skill sets required of successful leaders like Joe Reynolds. This book is a "tool chest" for good leaders who want to be better— and all who inevitably face unexpected challenges. Resilient leaders don't succeed simply by "hanging on" in the crucible of adversity. They must also be able to inspire those they lead through character, competence, and selflessness. The lessons here—taken to heart—will well serve you and those you lead.

Lt. Col. Oliver L. North, USMC (Ret.)

Host of "War Stories" on FOX News Channel
Author of the "American Heroes" book series

This Book Is Dedicated to "Leaders in the Arena"

I honor <u>leaders of character and competence</u>
across this great nation and beyond.

I honor <u>selfless servant leaders</u>
who lay down their lives for others.

I honor <u>leaders who set the conditions</u>
<u>for success</u> in others.

I honor <u>leaders who do not compromise</u>
in the toughest crucibles of leadership.

I honor <u>leaders who lead through crisis</u>:
restoring vision, purpose, and faith.

I honor <u>leaders who spend a lifetime honing their skills</u>
to serve others.

I honor <u>resilient leaders who stay the course</u>,
who run the race with excellence and endurance.

I honor <u>leaders who recognize that true wisdom</u>
<u>comes from above</u>.

I honor <u>leaders who help others bounce back</u>,
and higher than before.

Resilient Leaders is dedicated to the leader in each of us,
to the "Leader in the Arena."

May your tribe increase!

The Man in the Arena

By Teddy Roosevelt

Excerpt from the speech "Citizenship In A Republic"
delivered at the Sorbonne, Paris, France on April 23, 1910

"It is not the critic who counts;
not the man who points out how the strong man stumbles,
or where the doer of deeds could have done them better.

The credit belongs to the man who is actually in the arena,
whose face is marred by dust and sweat and blood;
who strives valiantly;
who errs, who comes short again and again,
because there is no effort without error and shortcoming;

but who does actually strive to do the deeds;
who knows great enthusiasms, the great devotions;
who spends himself in a worthy cause;
who at the best knows in the end the triumph of high
achievement,
and who at the worst, if he fails, at least fails while daring greatly,

so that his place shall never be
with those cold and timid souls who neither know victory nor
defeat."

Introduction
Leadership Makes a Difference!

Leadership is a contact sport. In the rough and tumble of life, leadership makes a difference. Excellent leadership (to which we aspire) integrates disciplines which ensure personal resilience, and promote resilience in others and in organizations.

In Book 1 of *The Resilience Trilogy*, *Resilient Warriors*, we established a solid foundation of resilience principles and practices. Now we move into a higher tier of consideration: How do I help others navigate the body slams of life? How do I help the organizations and people I lead recover from changing market conditions, tragic circumstances, perplexing dilemmas? How do I, as a leader, "give life?" How do I help people, teams, and entire organizations ride out the storms of life with values intact, restore function and enter into growth, and rebound to greater heights?

How do I do this, again and again? How do I stay the course? How do I bounce back, and how do I help others do the same?

My own life experiences as a leader in the military, business, non-profit ministry, and consulting have amply demonstrated the need for leader resilience. Certainly most of my time as a leader has been tremendously rewarding as the teams and organizations I have led experienced productiveness and prosperity. Yet, there have been times when I questioned if I could truly go on, times when I was about to go under, times when the pain and fog of trauma and tragedy made me want to hide. Frankly, there have been times when I wanted to quit. I know that my candor regarding the doubts and discouragements of leadership reflects what all leaders periodically feel and experience. Leaders get tired. Leaders get body slammed. Leaders also must bounce back, ideally even higher than before. Leaders must be resilient.

While on a recent visit to a military base to encourage troops and families, I spent time with a young officer who had worked for me in the past. He was getting ready to assume command of a battalion sized formation (roughly 700 troops) which would deploy to combat. In an unusual moment of candor for a military professional, he looked at me with tears in his eyes, soberly reflecting, "Sir, I don't know if I can get back in the saddle." This brave young officer, one of the finest leaders I have ever observed, had within the past year led another outfit in combat, experiencing significant loss of life and the associated trauma to families and fellow troopers. The weight of this leadership responsibility for human life and livelihood, the sustained press of constant vigilance, the frequent question, "Could I have done more?" (to save their lives), and the prospect of experiencing another "bloody deployment" had become almost overwhelming for this young leader, and for his wife and family.

It was clear that he had dipped very deeply into his well of courage. He was not sure if he could go on, yet he did. Through rest, reflection, the restorative power of personal faith, and an amazingly supportive family, he did get back in the saddle. He was uniquely equipped to provide life-giving leadership to a team which needed him. Because of his own resilience, he was now able to impart hope, courage, optimism, competence, and character to those he would lead through another round of noble accomplishments and numbing losses.

The resilience of this young leader has kept him in the fight, on behalf of the many who would conceivably perish without him. As importantly, his crucible leadership experiences are equipping him to lead thousands and tens of thousands. Having led and learned through challenging formative leadership experiences, this young leader will soon walk into a destiny of increased responsibility, service, and personal fulfillment, not unlike the good servant who properly stewarded his master's talents: *"'Well done, my good servant!' his master replied. 'Because you have been trustworthy in a very small matter, take charge of ten cities."* (Luke 19:17, NIV)

So what about you? Have you ever wanted to quit? Have you ever wanted to hide? Have you ever been pressed to the edge of personal integrity through anger, fatigue, or fear of failure? I venture to say that in your own marketplace of leadership (in the public or private sector, on the world stage or in the nursery, as a uniformed servant facing death daily or as one facing the daily monotony of shop life, in the complexities of a corporation or the high risk of small business ownership, or name your specific marketplace...), you can identify with most of these questions and challenges. I offer that you too sometimes wonder if you can get back in the saddle. I strongly suspect that resilience is a highly sought after quality for you as a leader, as it is for me and so many others.

Our journey together in *Resilient Leaders* will help you, help us, to be more resilient leaders and to promote resilience in those we serve. We will expand the theme that "Leadership is a Contact Sport," and discuss the reality and the role of "crisis" in the leadership equation. We will then cast the Resilience Life Cycle© (introduced in *Resilient Warriors*) in terms applicable to leaders, further dissecting the process into "Voice in the Dark!" (Leading Before Crisis), "Sir, We have a Situation!" (Leading During Crisis), and "I'd Rather Hide!" (Leading After Crisis). We will conclude with "Careful Your Well of Courage!" (Leader Self-Care) and a challenge to be a resilient leader, like Jesus. As with the other *Resilience Trilogy* books, we will visit numerous role models whose examples will equip and encourage leaders in every marketplace of life.

We will not shy away from the significant contribution of personal faith towards resiliency in leaders. In particular, we will amplify biblical truth where relevant and appropriate, as well as highlighting Jesus as "The Ultimate Resilient Leader". For those well familiar with the teachings of Jesus, you will benefit from the integration of biblical leadership truth into the complexities of your leadership marketplace. For those who may be unfamiliar with the Bible or the life of Jesus as a source of leadership wisdom (or perhaps even doubting the credibility of such an approach), I am confident that you will soon see the merits of "Leading Like Jesus" yourself, as you see the practical relevance that this servant leader from Galilee sets before us. You must certainly form your own opinion, but I personally conclude from decades of leading under a variety of highly demanding scenarios that the Bible is the "world's greatest leadership manual" and Jesus is the "world's greatest leadership role model." We will seek to fully tap these rich resources in order to reach our full potential as resilient leaders.

A final note before we begin another journey together: YOU are needed, needed as a leader, a resilient leader. Your family and friends need you to lead. Your community and nation need you to lead. Your world needs you to lead. This globe is a daunting place, a most challenging and complex environment which requires the best of leaders to make a difference. Whether you lead tens or tens of thousands, the difference you make will not be trivial. Such as the difference between Evil and Good. Or how about Poverty and Prosperity? Or Despair and Hope? Or Death or Life? Your life giving, resilient leadership can make the difference... it always does.

"Strap on, fellow leader"—we have some important work ahead of us.

1

Leadership: A Contact Sport

"Stop him! He's going to hurt him! Oh, no!!!" shouted my grandmother as she was watching Friday Night Wrestling, her very favorite show in the early days of TV. My "Granny," the normally genteel, white-haired, ninety-year-old matron saint of our family, would be particularly indignant when one wrestler would spin the other above his head like a helicopter blade, dramatizing the impending body slam onto the canvas. "Someone help him!" she would shout, but the outcome was always the same. The "victim" was mercilessly body slammed, yet would somehow recover (with Granny's ample encouragement) to continue the drama on behalf of the screaming audience at ringside and in "TV land." Along with the other wide-eyed grandchildren, I would follow Granny's lead as she vicariously entered into this dramatic struggle between good and evil; while the adults in the room would find great humor in Granny's utter belief in the antics of the wrestlers and her expressions of fright and indignation.

While now I know that the professional wrestlers of that day were often faking it for the benefit of entertainment, I also know that in the real world leaders don't get the luxury of faking it. The body slams that happen in their arena of leadership are very real. In golf terms, leaders in the real world seldom get to hit from "a good lie."

Conversely, the ball is usually behind a tree or in a divot, the wind is blowing, and your club grips are wet with rain or with sweat. You get the picture. Seldom do leaders have the luxury of working under ideal conditions with model subordinates, absolute clarity of the mission, total knowledge of the competitive forces they face, minimal infringement by outside factors, or even a clear awareness of one's own true capabilities or vulnerabilities.

Does this sound familiar?

Leaders <u>Will</u> Have Tribulation

As a reminder from the Book of John,

"In the world (of leadership), you (leaders) <u>will</u>
have tribulation..."
(John 16:33, NKJV, parenthetical comments and
underline added).

Applying a maxim from *Resilient Warriors* to each of us as leaders: "We (as leaders) are all at war, whether on the battlefront or the home front, whether in the board room or the class room. War is a reality for each of us (as leaders). We all take incoming." (*Resilient Warriors*, page 32, parenthetical comments added)

Yea verily, leaders take incoming, sometimes from the enemy and sometimes from friendlies. Leaders will have tribulation, trials, challenges, and body slams. Leadership truly is a contact sport!

Here is an example from the many "teachable moments" in my life as a leader:

"Eagle Six, this is Eagle Five. We have a situation, over."

"Roger, Five. What's your SITREP, over."

"Six, a bus carrying some of our battalion dependents rolled off a cliff. Multiple air medevacs (medical evacuations) in progress. Numerous serious injuries. Battalion Surgeon, Chaplain, and all available battalion medics en route. No known fatalities at this point, but still sorting it out. Location vicinity Checkpoint B. Request your ETA (estimated time of arrival). Over."

"Roger, Five. Request you inform Eagle 7, Eagle 3, and Mrs. Dees. I'll inform my higher. Moving now... ETA 5 minutes. Out."

Perhaps the shorthand communication above is foreign to you, or it may be very familiar to the military veteran reading this. Either way, you can easily identify these as those first haunting words of a crisis, a time when your mettle as a leader will be severely challenged, a time when the lives and deaths of others are literally in your hands. Such words may trigger you to remember your last crisis as a leader, or a parent, or as a follower.

By way of further explanation, as the incoming battalion commander of 1-8 Infantry (Fighting Eagles) at Fort Carson, Colorado, I was Eagle Six, the radio call sign. (For other radio call signs, Eagle Five = Battalion Executive Officer, Eagle Seven = Battalion Command Sergeant Major, Eagle 3 = Battalion Operations Officer, and "my higher" is the Brigade Commander, my boss.) "Mrs. Dees" is my dear bride, Kathleen, the "first lady" of the battalion whose passion was to support and empower the battalion's young military wives and families in every way possible.

As a new battalion commander, I was laser focused on intense training to standard in accord with the familiar Chinese proverb which exhorts, "We sweat in peace so we will not bleed in war." I also recognized the importance of families to the will and morale of our soldiers, and sought to turn family support into a battalion core competency as well.

Toward the end of my first six weeks in the field with the Fighting Eagles, we were conducting a "Family Day" with several hundred battalion families joining the battalion in a field location to see what "Dad" (no female soldiers in our infantry battalion ranks at this point) did "at work." Having participated in similar events in the past, I knew this type of event would be greatly appreciated by these young military families. This particular "Family Day" was proceeding well: sunny Colorado skies, outstanding food cooked up by the battalion mess sergeant and our great cooks, and lots of wide-eyed children, wives, and parents gaining greater respect and appreciation for the skills and sacrifice of their loved one engaged in military service. In short, a noble event on behalf of families, an ideal day, an almost completed mission of demonstrable care for our military families that would forge strong bonds for the tough training and operational missions the battalion would soon face.

Then it happened. Inexplicably (which is often how the description of an accident begins), a bus driver, transporting over 50 dependents ranging from a three-month old baby to an eighty-year-old grandmother of a soldier, veered too close to the soft shoulder of the dirt road and lost control. The bus rolled down the embankment, turning over three or four times.

When I arrived at the scene, I overlooked the unfolding drama with a pit in my stomach. In an area almost the size of a football field, hurt and traumatized dependents in a patchwork of little huddles dotted the terrain—a crouching medic applying bandages with another holding the IV (intravenous) bag of fluids, a chaplain praying with a cluster of shocked family members, a distraught parent of a bewildered young child who was wailing uncontrollably, and the heavy air of anger, despair, and hurt. I encouraged as many as possible, but quickly recognized that my "value add" as a leader would be to ensure that all available resources were brought to bear, to triage, console, and medevac the seriously injured to higher level medical capabilities at the Fort Carson Community Hospital. While I assisted the onsite coordination of the first medevac flights and gave instructions and information to battalion staff and subordinate unit commanders, I sent Kathleen and the Battalion Sergeant Major to the hospital where many family members were assembling to determine the status of their injured loved ones.

After the initial crisis was resolved (and gratefully, no one lost their lives), then began the strident assignment of blame by inflamed family members, the persistent media inquiries, and the threats of litigation by those who wanted to hold someone (or something) accountable for their pain. In fact, some accused me of "obviously not caring about them" because I was seemingly dispassionate as I was orchestrating the mass casualty evacuations. In these early days of command, I wanted to hide yet had an intuition that I absolutely must take the "slings and arrows" of these hurting people. I conducted a "town hall meeting" with interested parties and a press conference with local media, providing basic details, expressing regret for the incident and compassion for those impacted, and affirming the importance of military families to our overall mission.

We then re-intensified our collective efforts to turn this painful "obstacle" into an "opportunity" to excel at family support systems in the battalion. The Fighting Eagles were subsequently recognized for having one of the most innovative and effective family support programs at Fort Carson. The higher command investigation of the accident was daunting to a new battalion commander, yet turned into an expression of trust from senior commanders who quickly saw that my own personal introspection and corrective actions would be far more rigorous that the higher command might impose. In short, they saw they could trust me to lead the Fighting Eagles through this crisis, getting better and not bitter.

Thus unfolded a "crucible" leadership experience for young Lieutenant Colonel Bob Dees which would inform me for decades to come. While I will expand on these "lessons learned" in later sections of *Resilient Leaders*, let me highlight a few leadership realities and challenges in a complex and dangerous world:

- <u>Tragic accidents and circumstances happen under the supervision of good leaders doing the right thing for the right reasons</u>, just as "When bad things happen to good people" (referring to Harold Kushner's book by the same title). This is a reality in the unpredictable complexities of military leadership in war and peace, as well as in any other domain of public or private leadership.
- <u>Crisis defines the character of the Leader</u>. Crises shine a bright, penetrating light on the leader, revealing previously hidden weaknesses and strengths to self and others. Crises become "defining moments" between the leader and the led which cement relationships of trust and confidence needed for future challenges. Crises also define the true inclinations of your boss, sometimes revealing trust and confidence, or insecurity and control which become counterproductive to your efforts.
- <u>Hurting people often strike out at the nearest target or symbol of authority</u>. Leaders must understand this and

recognize the need to be a "heat shield" that graciously and securely absorbs the fiery darts from angry and disillusioned people and protects the organization and others from undue distraction to the mission.

- Despite the inclination to hide, leaders must use crises as "teachable moments" for themselves and others which accelerate learning, trust, and systemic improvements. The goal for the resilient individual, leader, and organization is to "bend and not break" as they recover, learn and adapt from crisis. "Good outfits talk to themselves," and it is the leader's responsibility to model such introspection for others.

This Fort Carson bus accident is but one of many vignettes I will provide throughout *Resilient Leaders* to illustrate the complex and challenging nature of leadership in the marketplaces of life. I suspect you have your own repository of "memorable" leadership situations, or soon will have as you lead people and organizations through challenging waters.

Fundamental Concepts: Resilient Leadership

Before closing this chapter with a final story, let's make sure we nail down some fundamental concepts regarding resilient leadership.

First, the essence of great leadership, resilient leadership, is Selfless Service over time from a platform of character (Chapters 2 and 3: Character Counts I and II) and <u>competence</u> (Chapters 4-9). The basis for this definition is Psalm 78:70-72 which describes the progression of King David as a leader. First, David demonstrated a servant's heart, starting in his lowly days helping with the sheep (sort of sounds like a plebe at West Point, or a young seaman in his early days at Great Lakes Naval Training):

"[70]He also chose David His servant and took him from the sheepfolds.

Then David progressed from *caring for sheep* to *caring for people* to *caring for the entire nation* of Israel.

"[71]From the care of the ewes with suckling Lambs He brought Him to shepherd Jacob His people, and Israel His inheritance.

And now the basis for our definition of great leadership:

"[72]So he shepherded them (Selfless Service)

According to the integrity of his heart, (character)

And guided them with his skillful hands." (competence)

> ...the essence of great leadership, resilient leadership, is <u>Selfless Service over time</u> from a platform of <u>character</u> and <u>competence</u>.

Jesus said it best when He deflated James and John who sought to be elevated above their fellow disciples:

"But it is not this way among you, but <u>whoever wishes to become great among you shall be your servant</u>; and whoever wishes to be first among you shall be slave of all. For even the Son of Man did not come to be served, but <u>to serve</u>, and <u>to give His life a ransom for many</u>." (Mark 10:43-45, underlines added)

Jesus well describes the essential nature of servant leadership in this passage, as well as providing numerous diverse and rich examples of selfless and resilient leadership throughout His life as a leader role model. In fact, Jesus will be one of our primary leadership mentors as we learn together about resilient leadership.

Secondly, the wording "over time" in our definition of great leadership implies a second essential ingredient: resilience. This means <u>leading with excellence *over time* through the realities of success and failure in the tough marketplaces of life</u>. It is the ability as a leader to bounce back from tough and perplexing leadership challenges, to help your team and your organization bounce back in similar fashion, and to do it repeatedly over time, without loss of passion or vision. *Resilient Leaders* takes the resilience paradigm laid forth in *Resilient Warriors* and applies these same principles of "bounce" to the world of leadership. We will examine this in significant depth in coming chapters.

> In the context of resilient leadership, resilience means leading with excellence *over time* through the realities of success and failure in the tough marketplaces of life.

When Least Expected

Within the Army command structure, company command is the first level. Although platoon leaders bear significant responsibility, company commanders are the first to truly experience "buck stops here" leadership (referring to President Harry S. Truman's famous phrase) as they grasp their first guidon, signifying the assumption of significant authority and responsibility.

I recall my first guidon. It was a blue pennant on a wooden staff with crossed Infantry rifles with "C" above and "2-503" below for "Hard Rock Charlie," Charlie company, 2d Battalion 503d Airborne Infantry. As the company executive officer, I was selected to command the company when Captain Marion Gerber had to leave command early for a family situation. We were in the field for the change of command, on top of a hill overlooking Kentucky Lake, a pristine area of wilderness west of Fort Campbell, Kentucky, where we were conducting training. The presiding 3d Brigade commander was Colonel (later Brigadier

General) "Tiger" Honeycutt whose nickname came from his Korean War exploits behind enemy lines to "snatch" enemy personnel for intelligence purposes. Having just put the company guidon into my hands, "Tiger" provided some challenging remarks to our assembled troops, received an update about our ongoing training, and then departed back to Fort Campbell in his command helicopter.

While I could still hear the "wop wop" of Colonel Honeycutt's departing UH-1 (Huey) helicopter, one of my former soldiers from the second platoon emerged sprinting from the wooded trail that meandered several hundred yards down to the water's edge.

"Frazier (name changed in sensitivity to family) is under the water. They can't find him!" shouted the winded runner.

Johnny Frazier had been my RTO (Radio Telephone Operator) when I was the second platoon leader six months prior. He was a strong, tall, red-haired, bright, gregarious kid from Alabama, a great soldier who had literally been my shadow for over a year, never more than a few feet away with his heavy PRC-77 radio, my communication lifeline to higher, lower, and adjacent units. We had climbed many a mountain together, and navigated the platoon through the dark of night to many an objective. Johnny's new platoon leader had decided to save some time by giving him a Ranger Swim Test in the murky waters of Kentucky Lake, rather than waiting for return to garrison and a test under more controlled conditions. During the course of the test, Johnny momentarily dropped under the water and his equipment snagged on an unseen branch in the water. His platoon leader and other helpers desperately tried to locate and rescue him under the water, yet they could not find him. Johnny Frazier, a vibrant young soldier with a bright future, drowned in a few short minutes. His was a tragic death, a needless loss. Johnny would never come "marching home again" (referring to popular Civil War song from the 1860s, "When Johnny Comes Marching Home Again").

Colonel "Tiger" Honeycutt, still en route back to Fort Campbell in his helicopter, received the initial "SIR" (serious incident report) on his command radio and returned to the LZ (landing zone) at our bivouac site which he had just departed. Now he looked at me through different eyes, asking many reasonable and very tough questions: "Why a swim test in Kentucky lake?" "Why no safety measures to mitigate the risk?" (lifeline, underwater reconnaissance, better communications, etc.) "What are you going to do now, Lieutenant Dees?" "You are the Commander."

I clearly recognized that the "authority" of command had just a few minutes before been placed in my hands, and now the "responsibility" of command was resting squarely on my shoulders. This was a teachable moment in the life of a young leader.

As is normal with a soldier fatality such as this, there was an Accident Review Board and an Article 15-6 investigation to establish findings and make recommendations regarding what judicial (Court Martial, similar to a Grand Jury hearing in the civilian world), non-judicial (Uniformed Code of Military Justice, Article 15), or administrative (such as a letter of reprimand) actions were warranted. Major Dan Campbell was the field grade 15-6 Officer assigned by the Tiger Honeycutt. After a rigorous investigation, the platoon leader was reprimanded with a career damaging letter and I was eventually exonerated. I was learning quickly about the principle of leader *accountability*.

While this story reinforces the leadership observations described earlier from the Fort Carson bus accident, this leader vignette also highlights other relevant takeaways:

- <u>Assumption of command is a clear defining moment when the challenge and privilege of command is transitioned into new hands</u>. The military command structure well understands this principle. "Unity of Command" is an important Principle of War (Clausewitz); confusion regarding who is ultimately calling the shots can be dysfunctional and deadly. The time honored "change of command" ceremony in the military is a very symbolic and practical way to "put the stick" of command into another's hands (Air Force vernacular for transitioning control of the aircraft to another pilot). Just as there cannot be two pilots-in-command (PIC), there cannot be multiple leaders at the top of an organization.

  While consensus decision making is a useful technique for a number of reasons, (such as noted in Proverbs 11:14, "Where there is no guidance the people fall, But in abundance of counselors there is victory"), the ultimate decider is a leader who has implied or specified responsibility, part of what is referred to as the "weight of command." A proper "succession of command" means the newly appointed leader is in charge, and the departing leader departs the scene, giving wide latitude to the new leader as he engages with his subordinate team, shapes new policies, and integrates his own personality and experience into the life of the organization. Although perhaps best understood in the military, these principles are applicable in every marketplace of life. The wise CEO, Board of Directors, and leader in every other walk of life do well to embrace them fully.

- Leaders with "Authority" to fulfill "Responsibility" are subject to "Accountability." I had been taught this principle many times over at West Point and in initial Infantry Officer Basic, but now I had lived it. When one "takes the guidon" of responsibility (or "takes the stick" as they would say in the Air Force), they are granted full authority with commensurate accountability for how they use that authority. A visible "succession of command" provides an important transition of authority, responsibility, and accountability. As incoming leaders grasp the guidon with confidence, commitment, and perhaps a significantly different approach to life and leadership, outgoing leaders who truly care for the organization rather than themselves must release their grip on unit activities and affections, moving on to future endeavors. Such clear and effective "leader succession" requires both character and competence on the part of all involved.

- Risk management (the discipline of identifying operational hazards and applying relevant controls to mitigate the associated risk) is a critical leader competency for leaders at all levels in all professions. One should not allow expediency to short circuit prudent measures to mitigate risk, while still training hard and maintaining tough, realistic standards. The ability to ASSESS risk, to emplace controls to MITIGATE risk, and to MONITOR changing risk factors are critical leadership skills. Each military Service as well as many other industrial sectors (construction, aviation, shipping, energy, et al) have very sophisticated systems for doing this.

Risk management is a mindset, equally applicable in more abstract areas such as relational risk. Senior leaders in particular must weigh (conduct a risk assessment of) the political and relational risks of their actions. While not being a "weathervane" subject to the latest opinion and popularity polls, the senior military leader, or business leader, or even parent of a teenager must realize that their decisions and stances present risks (to include risk to their personal and public relationships) that the wise leader will assess carefully. In a relational sense, tough decisions usually result in someone's "ox being gored," meaning someone will not be happy with the final decision. The wise senior leader learns to navigate such complexities without "burning more relational bridges" than necessary. As well, Chapter 3 will discuss emotional courage which involves "risking" close friendships which are key to long term leader success.

Risk management is an essential and learned competency for leaders of complex organizations operating in challenging and dangerous environments. While we have already noted that even great leaders can't always prevent bad outcomes, it is critical for leaders to develop a sixth sense regarding risk to the operation and the personnel which he oversees.

Gaining Altitude

To "gain altitude" as we close this chapter: leadership truly is a contact sport, but it is also one of the most rewarding of human endeavors, particularly when the leader has helped people believe in themselves and together accomplish what they thought impossible. We see these fulfilling aspects of leadership in every arena of life: on the sports field, in the board room, in families, churches, and communities, and on the battlefield. While leaders must expect tribulation, challenges, complexities, and downright "ugly" situations, they will often find that even these leadership morasses can have a positive ending as the resilient leader helps others navigate the storm to a safe landing and a productive future.

This defines great, resilient leaders. They make a positive difference in the lives of others, and they do it consistently over time.

> This defines great, resilient leaders. They make a positive difference in the lives of others, and they do it consistently over time.

We next turn to Chapter 2, "Character Counts I," to begin our foundational discussion of character in the leadership equation.

Resilient Leader Takeaways

RL 1 – Leadership is a contact sport. Expect tribulation.

RL 2 – In the rough and tumble of life, leadership makes a difference. Excellent leadership (to which we aspire) integrates disciplines which ensure personal resilience, and promote resilience in others and in organizations.

RL 3 – Resilient Leadership is Selfless Service over time from a platform of character and competence.

RL 4 – An essential ingredient of Resilient Leadership is leading with excellence *over time* through the realities of success and failure in the tough marketplaces of life.

RL 5 – Great, resilient leaders make a positive difference in the lives of others, and they do it consistently.

RL 6 – Good or great leadership is always preferred, but tragic accidents and circumstances frequently happen under the supervision of good leaders doing the right thing for the right reasons.

RL 7 – Crisis defines the character of the Leader.

RL 8 – Hurting people often strike out at the nearest target or symbol of authority. Leaders must understand this and recognize the need to be a "heat shield" that graciously and securely absorbs the fiery darts from angry and disillusioned people and protects the organization and others from undue distraction to the mission.

RL 9 – Leaders must use crises as "teachable moments" for themselves and others which accelerate learning, trust, and systemic improvements.

RL 10 – Assumption of command is a clear defining moment when the challenge and privilege of command is transitioned into new hands. A proper "succession of leadership" means the newly appointed leader is in charge, and the former leader departs the scene, giving wide latitude to the new leader as he engages with his subordinate team, shapes new policies, and integrates his own personality and experience into the life of the organization.

RL 11 – Leaders with "Authority" to fulfill "Responsibility" are subject to "Accountability."

RL 12 – Risk management is a critical leader competency for leaders at all levels in all professions. While great leaders can't always prevent bad outcomes, it is critical that every leader develop a sixth sense regarding risk to the operation and the personnel which he oversees.

Additional Study

1. Crocker III, H.W. *Robert E. Lee on Leadership.* Rocklin, CA: Prima Publishing, 1999.

2. Lockerbie, D. Bruce. *A Man Under Orders: LT. General William K. Harrison, Jr.* New York, NY: Harper & Row Publishers, 1979.

3. Barna, George. *Master Leaders.* Brentwood, TN: Tyndale House Publishers, 2009.

2

Character Counts I

Selflessness

"Above all the grace and gifts that Christ gives to His beloved
Is that of overcoming self."
Saint Francis of Assisi
1181-1226

"Prop blasts" in an airborne outfit are a "defining moment" for young lieutenants. A prop blast is the traditional celebration which is conducted when a new jumper just out of the U.S. Army Airborne School at Fort Benning, Georgia, has made his sixth jump with his newly-assigned unit (beyond his mandatory five jumps in airborne training). My prop blast came in March, 1973 soon after my assignment to the 2d Battalion 503 Airborne Infantry (2-503) in the 101st Airborne Division. As was typical in those days, the centerpiece of the prop blast ceremony was a drink from the "grog bowl." By most accounts this grog bowl tradition began with the westward expansion in the United States, when troopers would share their alcoholic spirits with one another in a communal brew which over time took on historical meaning with the addition of symbolic elements to depict unit history. In the Airborne community, the grog bowl is actually a steel pot with reserve parachute "ripcord" handles on both sides of the helmet, filled with a somewhat toxic concoction of various strong liquors, a dirty sock or two (representing the Infantry), sand (brown sugar) representing the beaches of Normandy, and other symbolic elements.   The ritual (at least as I experienced it) involves a simulated parachute jump, a hearty drink from the grog bowl, and a "PLF" (parachute landing fall) from a suitably high platform, often a table in the Officer's Club surrounded by cheering (and often quite inebriated) fellow officers of the battalion.

I was fourth in line, on top of a long table. As prop blast participants, we shuffled down the table as though part of an airborne "stick" moving toward the open door of a perfectly good airplane, holding our imaginary static lines above our heads. Each prop blast lieutenant would find himself in front of the very tall and intimidating battalion commander, Lieutenant Colonel Stanley Bonta, who was waiting with the grog at the exit end of the table. Grasping the handles, the young officer would take a big swig of grog (to the cheers of the approving audience), then do a good PLF off the table, roll back to his feet, come to attention to salute the Colonel, and depart in an airborne shuffle chanting, "Airborne, Airborne, Airborne."

Now it was my turn. I "stood in the door" on the edge of the table. Colonel Bonta handed me the helmet. A defining moment. I held the helmet high, rendered a hearty "Airborne, Sir," handed the untouched potion back to the somewhat surprised battalion commander, and then conducted an enthusiastic PLF off the table, rolled, saluted, and chanted "Airborne" across the finish line. The next lieutenant shuffled forward and the celebration continued. My "creative alternative" to drinking the grog went seemingly unnoticed, or so I thought.

While my "drink refusal" (analogous to the term "jump refusal" used for a jumper who refuses to go out the door of the plane) was not intended to be a commentary on the vices of excessive alcohol consumption or a judgmental statement based on deeply held religious beliefs, I did sense that, at least for rookie Second Lieutenant Bob Dees, "going with the flow" in the raucous prop blast would be a compromise of character. This conviction was no doubt a result of my formative experiences (physically, mentally, and spiritually) at West Point, some of which are described in *Resilient Warriors*.

Although my senior infantry leaders and fellow lieutenants never mentioned the incident to me, I soon noticed some surprising "consequences." Instead of the expected ridicule because I did not fully participate in the tribal prop blast, I soon found myself in increasing positions of trust and responsibility as a junior officer. Illustrative of this was the situation in Chapter 1 where I was entrusted with company command as a young lieutenant. I also found that my peers conferred new respect and often came to me when the chips were down in their own lives.

Apparently, my prop blast actions had been interpreted as an indicator of character and moral courage. Although I was just doing "what I thought was right," I saw that "Character Counts," particularly in a business where life and death decisions are the norm. Since those days as a young follower and leader, I have observed this principle many times over. Hence, it is fitting and proper for us to dwell on character as a critical ingredient of resilient servant leadership.

Recall that in Chapter 1 we defined servant leadership as "Selfless Service over time from a platform of character and competence." Let's begin to put texture to this definition by introducing the topic of CHARACTER, along with what my life experience suggests are the three "high core values" (a term used by Gus Lee in his excellent book, *Courage: The Backbone of Leadership*) of CHARACTER: SELFLESSNESS, INTEGRITY, and COURAGE.

Character Counts

The list of unprincipled leaders in the private and public sectors expands daily. The reality is that while competencies are important, character is the trump card. As an extreme case, Adolf Hitler possessed many outstanding leader competencies, but he clearly lacked character. It is a rare news day that does not give account of a leader whose weak character toppled a long list of credentials and competencies.

> The reality is that while competencies are important, character is the trump card.

John C. Maxwell makes this point well in *Talent is Never Enough*:

> "Many people with talent make it into the limelight, but the ones who have neglected to develop strong character rarely stay there long. <u>Absence of strong character eventually topples talent.</u> Why? Because people cannot climb beyond the limitations of their character. Talented people are sometimes tempted to take shortcuts. Character prevents that. Talented people may feel superior and expect special privileges. Character helps them to know better. Talented people are praised for what others see them build. Character builds what's inside them. Talented people have the potential to be difference makers. Character makes a difference in them. <u>Talented people are often a gift to the world. Character protects that gift.</u>" (page 191, underlines added)

While it is tempting to wind out with high profile examples of leaders whose absence of strong character has toppled their talent (just check the daily news), the reality is that each of us also have tangible (and painful) examples in our own immediate radius of action, or even in our own lives. Hence, we must all ask, "What is Character, and how do we ensure that it protects the talent, the competencies, and the full potential of our own lives and those we lead?"

If you do a brief Internet search for "CHARACTER," you will find hundreds of references that give an impressive variety of character traits, some listing under ten key traits as essential and others listing over 100. The vast majority of these websites, books, and other resources are very helpful; I wish I could absorb them all, and comment upon each in this book. For example, in *Courage: The Backbone of Leadership*, Gus Lee presents a useful framework of low core values, middle core values, and high core values. I will refer to this concept of "high core values" momentarily.

> My singular task in *Resilient Leaders* is to be a messenger to you of those leader qualities of character and competence that God burned into my psyche and soul through the leadership crucibles I navigated in the military and beyond.

While your crucible experiences will be different than mine, my prayer is that you will benefit from the principles and examples given. I certainly would have benefited from a book such as *Resilient Leaders* to inform and motivate my early days as a young leader and as a continual reminder during the ascent into ever increasing leadership opportunities and challenges.

From my perspective and life experience, the three "high core values" of CHARACTER are Selfless Service, Integrity, and Courage.

Selfless Service

Selfless Service lies at the heart of effective leadership. We often use the term "servant leader" to emphasize the importance of this characteristic. Selfless Service is a core value for all the military services, inculcated from the early days of indoctrination with both officers and enlisted. The U.S. Army defines Selfless Service in the following way:

> **"Put the welfare of the Nation, the Army and your subordinates before your own.** Selfless service is larger than just one person. In serving your country, you are doing your duty loyally without thought of recognition or gain. The basic building block of selfless service is the commitment of each team member to go a little further, endure a little longer, and look a little closer to see how he or she can add to the effort."

As well, Selfless Service is highly valued in the public and private sectors of government and business. It is a true American value, without which we forfeit compassion, entrepreneurial spirit (versus self absorption with entitlements), strength, vitality, and moral authority as a nation. As an example, President John F. Kennedy at his inaugural address on January 20, 1961 exhorted United States' citizens to "...ask not what your country can do for you—ask what you can do for your country."

In similar fashion, President Ronald Reagan, for veteran's observances in November, 1981, reflected, "The willingness of our citizens to give freely and unselfishly of themselves, even their lives, in defense of our democratic principles, gives this great Nation continued strength and vitality."

Jesus was also very clear on the subject of Selfless Service when He responded to the request from the mother of James and John that her sons be exalted to the right and left hand of Jesus when He comes into glory:

> "For even the Son of Man did not come to be served, but <u>to serve, and to give His life a ransom for many</u>." (Mark 10:45, underline added)

Most importantly, Jesus' actions matched his words, ultimately giving His very life for others. This is how you and I are also challenged to lead.

In its simplest form, Selfless Service is "serving others without regard for self" and inherently includes personal sacrifice. Selfless Service is hard, not natural for most of us who are generally wired to look out for "Number 1." Selfless Service can be developed over time: for some it begins at an early age in the home, some "catch" the spirit of Selfless Service from the example and sacrifice of other selfless leaders, and others may begin to learn Selfless Service at institutions such as our nation's military academies or at military basic training. Some leaders, however, never get it, rising to high levels of influence under the false impression that it is "all about them." Gratefully, in the military at least, most leaders "who don't get it" are weeded out before they reach high levels of command.

> In its simplest form, Selfless Service is
> "serving others without regard for self"
> and inherently includes personal sacrifice.

In *Leadership above the Line,* Dr. Sarah Sumner adds an additional complexity to this consideration of Selfless Service. She makes the important point that our strongest positive characteristics can also become our greatest shortcomings. She counsels "leadership above the line" which captures the positive benefits of a certain personal characteristic while minimizing the downsides. For example, she suggests that the personal qualities that make highly effective strategists discerning, analytical, clear communicators, etc., can also make this same strategist self-righteous, harsh, and impatient. I have likewise observed this many times in my own life and in others: often our greatest strengths, when applied with selfish motives, can become our greatest excesses and weaknesses. From my perspective, the "line" Dr. Sumner addresses is the boundary between selfless leadership ("above the line," applying one's talents with proper and noble motives) versus selfish leadership ("below the line," using one's competencies for self-serving purposes and narcissistic gratification).

In *Courage: The Backbone of Leadership* (page 108), Gus Lee highlights selflessness through a vignette about then Major

Norman Schwarzkopf, the future four-star commander of Operation Desert Shield/Desert Storm who would lead the liberation of Kuwait from the grasp of an unprovoked invasion by Saddam Hussein's Iraq. While an instructor at West Point, Major Schwarzkopf gave then West Point cadet Gus Lee and his fellow students a leadership quandary to resolve and then provided the following concise explanation of the difference between selfish and selfless leaders:

> "'There are two kinds of people in the world: leaders and careerists. Leaders have character. They act for what is right. They would die for their men.' His words sank into the chalkboards, the walls, us.

> 'Careerists,' he said, making the word sound like a crime against God, 'are self-centered, self-absorbed. They act out of selfishness. They sacrifice their men for a promotion. They lie to pump up results. They save their skins instead of others. Careerists can't really lead because their men do not trust them and will not willingly follow.'"

I include myself among those for whom Selfless Service did not come naturally, who entered the military with a careerist mindset. Reflecting back on my early days as a young Army lieutenant, I had lots of great checklists from my leadership instruction at West Point and beyond, but I cannot truly say I was serving others for the right reasons. More often than not, I was self-serving. Along the way, however, I saw soldiers sacrifice their personal comfort and their very lives for others. I saw military families silently suffer, yet continue to love and support their soldier. Somewhere along the way, the mental checklists started to move into my heart. "Take care of the troops" became more than just a bumper sticker; it became a heartfelt passion and eventually a divine calling as a leader.

As I grew spiritually during my formative years as a leader, I also recognized that Selfless Service is the central tenet of Biblically-based leadership, particularly demonstrated by the life and leadership of Jesus. As a young Christian leader, I was fortunate to have many selfless servant role models: Cleo Buxton, Reverend Andy Seidel, Reverend Paul Pettijohn, Lieutenant General William K. Harrison, Lieutenant General Howard Graves, Major General Clay Buckingham, Colonel Al Shine, Colonel Dick Kail, Lieutenant Colonel Tom Hemingway, and so many others who modeled Jesus on behalf of those they led and served.

Wrapped in a less spiritual package, but likewise instructive and motivating, was the leadership mentoring from greats such as Generals "Tiger" Honeycutt, Saint, Palmer, Crouch, Reimer, Jaco, Shalikashvili, Schwartz, and Wallace, as well as business leaders such as Doug Armstrong at Electronic Warfare Associates and Mitra Azizirad, Curt Kolcun, and Teresa Carlson at Microsoft.

Equally important, I was blessed with a selfless Christian wife, Kathleen, who modeled Selfless Service for me in many ways as we grew together in the service of God, nation, and others. These role models have been the "picture worth a thousand words."

Maybe you can also identify with this progression from mental assent, to heartfelt compassion, to divine calling to serve others at the expense of self. Maybe you also can identify great role models of selfless servant leaders. Or maybe as you consider your own leadership motivations and models, you must candidly admit that you are not there yet.

> Maybe you can also identify with this progression from mental assent to heartfelt compassion, to a divine calling to serve others at the expense of self...
> Or maybe you are not there yet.

Selfless Service in Action

Jesus taught about <u>Selfless Service in the parable of the Good Samaritan</u> recorded in Luke 10:25-37. As Jesus was teaching, He was challenged by a clever lawyer seeking to entrap him. This passage is worth dissecting.

> [25] And a lawyer stood up and put Him to the test, saying, "Teacher, what shall I do to inherit eternal life?" [26] And He said to him, "What is written in the Law? How does it read to you?" [27] And he answered, "YOU SHALL LOVE THE LORD YOUR GOD WITH ALL YOUR HEART, AND WITH ALL YOUR

SOUL, AND WITH ALL YOUR STRENGTH, AND WITH ALL YOUR MIND; AND YOUR NEIGHBOR AS YOURSELF." [28] And He said to him, "You have answered correctly; DO THIS AND YOU WILL LIVE."

Note above that Jesus answered with what is conventionally called The Great Commandment, and the basis we use in *Resilient Warriors* (page 172) for Comprehensive Personal Fitness™ (physical, mental, spiritual, emotional, and relational health). Now the lawyer sought to deflect Jesus' focus on this call to Selfless Service:

[29]But wishing to justify himself, he said to Jesus, "And who is my neighbor?"

[30] Jesus replied and said, "A man was going down from Jerusalem to Jericho, and fell among robbers, and they stripped him and beat him, and went away leaving him half dead. [31] And by chance a priest was going down on that road, and when he saw him, he passed by on the other side. [32] Likewise a Levite also, when he came to the place and saw him, passed by on the other side."

This is a tragic sight under any circumstances, whether in ancient Israel or on the streets of major cities in the U.S., or around the world. Someone in great need, yet most pass by "on the other side," refusing to engage. Notably the two who passed in this story were "professionals" (a priest and a Levite) who were unwilling to be inconvenienced, unwilling to show compassion, more concerned with self than service.

And now our selfless servant arrives:

> [33] But a Samaritan, who was on a journey, came upon him; and when he saw him, he felt compassion, [34] and came to him and bandaged up his wounds, pouring oil and wine on *them*; and he put him on his own beast, and brought him to an inn and took care of him.

This Good Samaritan "felt compassion," he acted upon that compassion by providing immediate medical care for his wounds (and no doubt emotional support in the process), and he transported the beaten man to a safe location and took care of him. He did not care about what others would think, or about the consequences to himself: he simply did what was right.

Then, the Good Samaritan went "the extra mile" and truly demonstrated Selfless Service, giving of his own resources (two days wages with a commitment to pay more if needed) to provide continuing care for the victim:

> [35] On the next day he took out two denarii and gave them to the innkeeper and said, "Take care of him; and whatever more you spend, when I return I will repay you."

Finally, Jesus drives the point home. The one of those passing by who "showed mercy toward him" was the true selfless servant. Jesus challenges the questioner to lay aside his theoretical arguments about "who is my neighbor" to embrace the practical application ("Go and do the same") of Selfless Service:

[36] Which of these three do you think proved to be a neighbor to the man who fell into the robbers' hands? [37] And he said, "The one who showed mercy toward him." Then Jesus said to him, "Go and do the same."

And the challenge conveys to each of us as well:

Will we serve others without regard for self?

What does being a "Good Samaritan" look like in our particular marketplace… or in our family… or in our community?

Who is "our neighbor" as leaders? It is those we lead.

May we "Go and do the same."

Selflessness Drives Motives

Before departing the subject of Selfless Service, it is important for us to be candid about the motives of the leader which drive "why we do what we do."

The proper motives of the leader directly spring from a spirit of Selfless Service. In my own leadership experience, I observed (and felt) a transformation in my underlying motives for my actions as a leader, but this occurred over a number of years. As mentioned earlier, I came out of West Point with a lot of good training (both military and spiritual), yet I was certainly not yet a servant leader. A real gut check in this area was my first "IG" inspection as a company commander. "IG" stands for Inspector General, the role of one in the military command structure to assist the command with enforcement of standards and to investigate serious breaches in those standards. In general terms, the IG is an intimidating person, particularly for young officers and non-commissioned officers (NCOs) who are quick to please and anxious to "look good." Gratefully in a military at war, significant issues of readiness and troop/family support come to the fore. In the post-Vietnam days, however, command inspection programs (CIPs) often took on a life of their own, often being a primary event which would determine how a young commander was evaluated on his OER (Officer Efficiency Report).

This was the case in 1976 when I was the company commander for B Company, 3d Battalion 187th Infantry in the 101st Airborne Division (Air Assault). With an upcoming IG Inspection, we prepared for months to "look good." Certainly much of the preparatory effort was well placed, allowing us to improve systems, uncover areas we had neglected, and enhance readiness. Yet, I now recognize that too much of our efforts were aimed at "spit and polish." I also recognized that as a commander, I was the primary one who placed inappropriate emphasis upon how things looked versus how things truly were. In essence, I overemphasized form over substance, and my underlying motive was to make Bob Dees look good.

When the week of the IG inspection arrived, I was really "wired," anxious to receive a good inspection report which would be reviewed by commanders above me, including my former brigade commander (remember the drowning story) and recent boss (I served as his Aide-de-Camp), Brigadier General "Tiger" Honeycutt, who was still in position as the Assistant Division Commander for Operations of the 101st. My subordinate leaders and energetic solders in the company ensured that we passed the inspection with flying colors. B/3-187 looked great!

Yet the victory was hollow. In my "heart of hearts," I knew that we had focused on the wrong things. We had done things right, but we (particularly me as the leader) had not done the right things for the right reasons. This was an important early experience to reveal to me my true (and rather shallow and self-serving) motives as a leader.

> The proper motives of the leader
> directly spring from a spirit of Selfless Service.

This progression of a leader's true motives may be instructive for you; I alluded to it earlier. Coming out of West Point as a young leader, I had many checklists in my head which included the twin maxims "accomplish the mission and take care of the troops." My motives were driven by my head knowledge to follow the checklist. Somewhere along the way, however, the seat of motivation seemed to move from my head to my heart, and eventually was burned deeply into my soul as a divine calling. I'm not sure exactly when this happened. Maybe it was when I saw soldiers die for one another, for a noble cause, or needlessly. Maybe it was when I saw the "great stroller brigades" and "bakers of cookies" (referring to wives/husbands and young children who so passionately support their beloved soldiers) lined up to provide a last cheer as their soldier departs to harm's way, perhaps never to return again. Maybe it was as I learned more about the life and example of Jesus, appreciating His "divine call" and sacrifice for me and others. While I can't pinpoint a time or event, I can say that the gradual transformation of my motives as a leader was critical to my effectiveness and resilience. I trust that you are on that same journey.

Permit me a short Biblical excursion which highlights the same principle. You may recall from *Resilient Warriors* the primary resilience passage of the Bible:

> "...we are afflicted in every way, but not crushed; perplexed, but not despairing; persecuted, but not forsaken; struck down, but not destroyed; always carrying about in the body the dying of Jesus, so that the life of Jesus also may be manifested in our body." (2 Corinthians 4:8-10)

The verse which immediately precedes this resilience passage places appropriate emphasis on leader motives and relates these motives to the resilience passage above:

> "But we have this treasure in earthen vessels, <u>so that the surpassing greatness of the power will be of God and not from ourselves</u>." (Verse 7, underline added)

A little explanation is in order. The historical context here is that in Biblical times, people would take "old cracked pots" and cover the outside with beeswax, making them look bright and shiny on the outside. This practice, akin to the façades we have discussed earlier, covered the cracks, at least until the bright sun melted the beeswax and the cracks reappeared.

This story relates to leader vulnerability, candor, and humility. Certainly there is a balance between candor and discretion, as well as confidence and humility as a leader, but young leaders are often motivated to "cover the cracks." The reality is that when mounting responsibility and complexity bring greater heat and pressure into the life of leaders, the cracks show anyway (the "wax" of facades melts, despite any efforts to look good). Young leaders (in every walk of life) do well to appreciate this principle early in their careers, allowing themselves to be real and credible to their followers, rather than acting out a "plastic superman" charade which will come to a halt when reality crashes onto the scene.

Gaining Altitude

We continue this investigation of CHARACTER into the next Chapter: Character Counts II. We have seen the centrality of SELFLESS SERVICE. Now we look at INTEGRITY and COURAGE to complete discussion of our three "high core values" of CHARACTER: a three strand cord (Selfless Service, Integrity, and Courage) that is not easily broken ("And if one can overpower him who is alone, two can resist him. A cord of three strands is not quickly torn apart." Ecclesiastes 4:12).

Resilient Leader Takeaways

RL 13 – While competencies are important, character is the trump card.

RL 14 – Selfless Service, Integrity, and Courage form a three strand cord of Character that is not easily broken.

RL 15 – Selfless Service is "serving others without regard for self" and inherently includes personal sacrifice.

RL 16 – Resilience in leadership means leading with excellence *over time* through the realities of success and failure in the tough marketplaces of life.

RL 17 – The proper motives of the leader directly spring from a spirit of Selfless Service.

RL 18 – Maybe you can also identify with this progression from mental assent, to heartfelt compassion, to divine calling to serve others at the expense of self…. Or maybe you are not there yet.

Additional Study

1. Sumner, Sarah. *Leadership Above the Line*. Carol Stream, IL: Tyndale House Publishers, 2006.

2. http://biblegateway.com. I recommend you do topical studies on key words such as courage, integrity, sacrifice, and service. Diving deeply into the Biblical examples of these key character traits will provide a new depth, perspective, and inspiration.

3. Maxwell, John C. *Talent is Never Enough*. Nashville, TN: Thomas Nelson, 2007.

3

Character Counts II
Integrity and Courage

"Failure is seldom fatal,
Success is seldom final,
It is courage that counts."
Winston Churchill

At the conclusion of Chapter 2, we summarized that Selfless Service, Integrity, and Courage form a three strand cord of Character that is not easily broken. Now we discuss INTEGRITY and COURAGE.

Integrity of the Leader

Adding to Selfless Service, Integrity is another high core quality of character that most would cite as essential. Let us look at integrity on several levels.

At the basic level, integrity is simply telling the truth or staying true to a set of values. As plebes at West Point, we received countless hours of indoctrination regarding the honor code:

> "A cadet does not lie, cheat, or steal, or tolerate others who do."

Certainly this maxim of not telling a lie is fundamental, but this is only the beginning of integrity.

> "...not telling a lie is fundamental, but this is only the beginning of integrity."

A dictionary definition of integrity from *Merriam-Webster* (bold inserted) includes the following:

> 1: firm adherence to a code of especially moral or artistic values: **incorruptibility**
> 2: an unimpaired condition: **soundness**
> 3: the quality or state of being complete or undivided: **completeness**

As well, the Army defines Integrity as one of its seven core values:

> **"Do what's right, legally and morally.** Integrity is a quality you develop by <u>adhering to moral principles</u>. It requires that you <u>do and say nothing that deceives others</u>. As your integrity grows, so does <u>the trust others place in you</u>. The more <u>choices you make based on integrity</u>, the more this highly prized value will affect your relationships with family and friends, and, finally, the fundamental acceptance of yourself." (underlines added)

These are certainly good definitions of integrity, but let me expand with a couple of important analogies. In mathematics, "integration" is the aggregation of effect over time, distance, or some other criteria. For example, if one integrates force over time, the end result is "work." Integration is a powerful mathematical tool, allowing one to calculate combined effect. I'll let you connect with your favorite mathematician friend if you want to explore this analogy more.

One other analogy would be from my Navy friends who often refer to "watertight integrity" on a ship. In essence, each compartment on a ship is "watertight" so that the impact of flooding is mitigated by the capability to seal off each compartment and reduce the likelihood of catastrophic flooding and likely sinking. This principle would highlight the importance of safeguarding every area of our life to reduce the overall impact of "flooding." Specifically, how do we identify potential threats in our lives as leaders? How do we quickly seal off and deal with leadership issues and personal impropriety before they invade and swamp our entire life?

This concept of compartmentalization to achieve watertight integrity may seem contradictory to the spirit of full integration, but they are actually complementary. For a Navy ship to achieve maximum effectiveness it has a labyrinth of passageways and communications means to ensure that the ship operates as a single entity. Yet, when a threat to the integrity of the ship is imminent, there are mechanisms to seal off the potential damage. So it is with each of us as leaders. Our lives need full integration across the broad range of faith, family, and profession, but when a threat does arise, integrity also requires that we quickly identify the problem, seal off the broader impacts, and address the personal or corporate issue. I'll let you connect with your favorite Navy friend to dive deeper (sorry the pun!) into this useful analogy.

Our lives need full integration across the broad range of faith, family, and profession, but when a threat does arise, integrity also requires that we quickly identify the problem, seal off the broader impacts, and address the personal or corporate issue.

Integrity in Action

During the late 1980s, I was working in the Pentagon, living outside the DC beltway (alluding to the highway beltway that surrounds the National Capitol Region in Washington, D.C.) in Burke, VA, and worshipping at our home church, Burke Community Church. At the same time, I was the Officer's Christian Fellowship area coordinator for the National Capitol Region, laboring conceptually with how military professionals who daily commuted to a high-pressure Pentagon job could keep their lives on track with their Lord and others. I observed military personnel who would "Praise the Lord" on Sunday in church, but would talk like drunken sailors on Monday in their workplace cubicle in the Pentagon. As well, their interactions with spouse, children, and others were often compartmented into even another realm of their lives. I nicknamed this phenomenon "Beltway Schizophrenia."

What was this all about? How do these military professionals avoid compartmented, fragmented, segregated lifestyles? How do they maintain their character, their integrity, in the workplace where they spend most of their waking hours? I came to the conclusion that living one's faith in the workplace was far more essential to overall integrity than I had appreciated. Military professionals, just like business men and women and leaders in every walk of life, need to "walk the walk" of personal faith in their workplace in order to truly live "integral lives" and to tap the full power of faith as they seek excellence in the workplace.

> I came to the conclusion that living one's faith in the workplace
> was far more essential to overall integrity
> than I had appreciated.

Applying these concepts of mathematical integration and watertight integrity to leadership and balanced living, a broader definition of integrity is, "A seamless integration of faith, family, and profession into a God-honoring life message."

While the application of this principle might be different for each of us, its importance is unmistakable. A relevant faith informs all that we do; certainly in our place of worship and spiritual learning, but also on the "playing fields of life" with particular emphasis on family and profession. This is what integrity on a higher plane looks like in the life of a leader: the seamless integration of faith, family, and profession into a God-honoring life message.

> Integrity on a higher plane is the
> seamless integration of faith, family, and profession
> into a God-honoring life message.

One more comment regarding integrity. It is difficult work for the leader to carry façades, "heat shields" against personal vulnerability and candor with others. This façade bearing becomes even more difficult and tiring as one rises to higher levels of responsibility and visibility. Certainly leaders must value discretion and always demonstrate respect for others, but the common workplace tendency is to keep your shield up and present a public "persona" that may be quite unlike your private persona with God and others.

Often when a highly visible leader has a personal slip in character, the debate resurfaces whether a leader's private actions influence his public service. Although not accepted by our popular culture, the answer is indisputable: character, particularly integrity, counts across the entire spectrum of our lives as leaders. My observation over many years is that integration of faith, family, and profession across both the public and private domains of one's life allows the busy and often weary leader to minimize the need for façades, to reduce the energy drain of "trying to be someone you are not." Such integrity is essential to staying power and resilience in leaders.

To close this section on integrity, let us return to the foundational description of King David's leadership in Psalm 78:72 (parenthetical notations and italics added):

"So he shepherded them (Selfless Service)

According to the integrity of his heart, (character)

And guided them with his skillful hands." (competence)

While many other leader characteristics could possibly have been cited here, David was highlighted for his INTEGRITY. May this also be true for you and me as resilient leaders, "leading with excellence over time through the realities of success and failure in the tough marketplaces of life."

Courage of the Leader

Whenever I need a little courage, a little "steel in my backbone," I often turn to Medal of Honor Citations. Each one is amazing. Each one illustrates extraordinary physical courage, undergirded by so many other qualities of character. For example, consider the account of one of the most beloved "Rakkasans" (187th Regimental Combat Team, Korean War), Corporal Rodolfo P. "Rudy" Hernandez, now 81 years old, and still an inspiration to so many:

> *"Corporal Hernandez, a member of Company G, distinguished himself by <u>conspicuous gallantry and intrepidity above and beyond the call of duty</u> in action against the enemy. His platoon, in defensive positions on Hill 420, came under ruthless attack by a numerically superior and fanatical hostile force, accompanied by heavy artillery, mortar, and machine gun fire which inflicted numerous casualties on the platoon. His comrades were forced to withdraw due to lack of ammunition <u>but Cpl. Hernandez, although wounded in an exchange of grenades, continued to deliver deadly fire into the ranks of the onrushing assailants until a ruptured cartridge rendered his rifle inoperative</u>. Immediately leaving his position, <u>Cpl. Hernandez rushed the enemy</u> armed only with rifle and bayonet. <u>Fearlessly engaging the foe</u>, he killed 6 of the enemy before falling unconscious from*

grenade, bayonet, and bullet wounds but <u>his heroic action momentarily halted the enemy advance and enabled his unit to counterattack and retake the lost ground</u>. The indomitable fighting spirit, <u>outstanding courage</u>, and tenacious devotion to duty clearly demonstrated by Cpl. Hernandez reflect the highest credit upon himself, the infantry, and the U.S. Army." (underlines added)

Certainly we could draw further inspiration from other Medal of Honor citations, or from September 11, 2001 heroes like Todd Beamer and his courageous comrades on Flight 93 ("Let's Roll"), or so many courageous New York City firemen charging up the Twin Towers with certain knowledge they would never return, or from our troops of today who charge into harm's way with unfailing courage, or their families who demonstrate the same. Such demonstrations of valor often say it all: selflessness, integrity, and certainly courage.

While these examples provide the picture worth a thousand words, further discussion is warranted. What is Courage? How do we "take courage" (as so often exhorted in the Scriptures)? What fearful obstacles are really "cleverly disguised opportunities" to display courage? What does courage look like across the elements of Comprehensive Personal Fitness™ (physical, mental, spiritual, emotional, and relational)?

Definitions of Courage

First, let us look at a few definitions of courage:

The U.S. Army highlights the physical and moral dimensions of "personal courage" in a very clear and practical way:

> **"Face fear, danger or adversity (physical or moral).** Personal courage has long been associated with our Army. With physical courage, it is a matter <u>of enduring physical duress and at times risking personal safety</u>. Facing moral fear or adversity may be <u>a long, slow process of continuing forward on the right path, especially if taking those actions is not popular with others</u>. You can <u>build your personal courage by daily</u> standing up for and acting upon the things that you know are honorable."

Slightly different from the Army definition, the *Merriam-Webster Dictionary* does not refer to courage as a physical quality, but suggests that courage is "mental or moral strength to venture, persevere, and withstand danger, fear, or difficulty."

One more insight regarding the definition of courage comes from the Johnson O'Connor *English Vocabulary Builder*:

> "The word COURAGE goes back through Old French to the Latin, *cor*, <u>heart</u>. Originally in English COURAGE meant heart, mind, thought. It has

come to mean <u>valor, boldness, bravery</u>; but it still carries the idea of <u>an intelligent approach, resolution</u>, and in this sense is an exact opposite of TEMERITY, which is thoughtless daring, fool-hardiness." (underlines added)

In his seminal book called *Courage: The Backbone of Leadership* (page 201), Gus Lee summarizes well:

"Courage is <u>facing fear rather than denying it</u>; it is rushing forward to face the problem, to <u>confront the giant whose shadow looms larger in our imagination than in reality</u>.

"It is fiercely exercising the <u>daily disciplines of courageous behavior</u> and consciously <u>rejecting the gradual immersion into cycles of poor behaviors</u>, stress-driven decisions, and anxious relationships.

"Even better, <u>you can grow your courage</u> to become a person of strength and character without waiting for a dramatic and life-changing incident. <u>Every day we receive new opportunities to demonstrate courage for others</u>.

"This begins with the <u>courage to change behaviors</u>. It ends with our commitment to <u>accountability for those changes</u>."

A common thread in all these definitions is that courage is facing down fear. This reminds us of the "equation" we used in *Resilient Warriors*: "FEAR + FAITH = COURAGE." (page 124) To further support this concept, we bring to mind another Biblical passage that addresses FAITH as the bridge between FEAR and COURAGE:

> "[15] Whoever confesses that Jesus is the Son of God (FAITH), God abides in him, and he in God... [17] By this, love is perfected with us, so that we may have confidence in the day of judgment; because as He is, so also are we in this world. [18] <u>There is no fear in love (FEAR); but perfect love casts out fear (COURAGE)</u>..." (1 John 4:15-18, underline and parentheses added)

Again we see the power of FAITH which leads to perfect love which casts out FEAR. Result: COURAGE. God-given love for others and love for a higher cause is generally a common denominator in heroism. In essence, warriors seldom perform great acts of courage for their flag alone, but they do fight ferociously and courageously for their battle buddies next to them and for their loved ones on the home front.

> FAITH is the bridge which leads from FEAR to COURAGE.

Likewise, Jesus Himself often pointed his followers to COURAGE. In *Resilient Warriors* we became familiar with a capstone verse which highlights the reality of tribulation and the provision of COURAGE.

"These things I have spoken to you, so that in Me you may have peace. In the world you have tribulation, <u>but take courage</u>; I have overcome the world." (John 16:33, underline added)

Ultimately, personal identification with Jesus (who has overcome the world) allows each of us to truly "take courage."

Summarizing key takeaways from these definitions before we dive into further discussion, we conclude the following:

- Courage is a learned behavior which increases each time we stare down fear.
- Courage must be balanced with selflessness and integrity.

Courage is the cumulative result of facing down fear across the full spectrum of the physical, mental, spiritual, emotional, and relational domains.

A Comprehensive Look at Courage

As with INTEGRITY, COURAGE is a high core quality of CHARACTER that is essential to excellent leadership over time, essential to being a resilient leader. Out of many attributes that Moses could have reinforced when he commissioned Joshua as the new leader of Israel in Deuteronomy 31:23, he simply said "Be strong and courageous." He did not say "Be strong and smart"... or honest... or loyal... or honorable... or many other important traits that Moses could have mentioned. He said "Be strong and courageous."

So it comes "full circle" back to US. How are we strong and courageous? What are the ways we demonstrate courage over time in the daily dilemmas of life and leadership, as well as courageous acts in those "seconds of sheer terror" that sometimes invade our world? What does such courage look like across the domains of Comprehensive Personal Fitness™: Physical, Mental, Spiritual, Emotional, and Relational?

Physical Courage

- <u>Fear of imminent bodily harm</u> to self or others such as David's reference in Psalm 91:5 to "the terror by night, or the arrow that flies by day." ('Sounds like incoming tracers in the dark, IED's, and snipers to me) (PHYSICAL)

One of David's "mighty men" in the scriptures named Benaiah modeled physical courage against such fears; he proved courageous in many defining moments. As it says in 2 Samuel 23:20,

> "Then Benaiah the son of Jehoiada, the son of a valiant man of Kabzeel, who had done mighty deeds, killed the two sons of Ariel of Moab. <u>He also went down and killed a lion in the middle of a pit on a snowy day</u>." (underline added)

Certainly Benaiah demonstrated bravery when killing two men in hand-to-hand combat, but this "lion thing" really caught my eye. Can you imagine going into a slippery, snowy pit to kill a lion? In his powerful book *In a Pit With a Lion On a Snowy Day*, Mark Batterson highlights that this physical bravery of Benaiah was the result of many small acts of preparation:

> "In a sense, Benaiah's heroic acts of courage were unplanned. But don't think that Benaiah was unprepared. He couldn't predict when, how, or where the lion encounter would happen, but he had been preparing for it since he was a boy. Can't you see Benaiah wrestling with his poor pet cat that doubled as an imaginary lion? He practiced his swordsmanship in front of a mirror until it became second nature. And he staged faux battles with his brothers. So when the lion crossed his path he didn't see it as *bad luck*. He saw it for what it was: *a divine appointment*. He literally seized the opportunity. The lion didn't take Benaiah by surprise. He had been waiting for it his entire life." (page 135)

Mark Batterson also uses Benaiah as a bridge to discuss other dimensions of courage in our lives. In essence, he challenges us all to be "lion chasers," chasing our hopes, dreams, aspirations, our full potential in God to selflessly overcome fear to do the right thing on behalf of others. These less tangible forms of courage also take a lifetime of preparation. Eleanor Roosevelt said it well,

"You gain strength, courage, and confidence by every experience in which you really stop to look fear in the face."

We should certainly train and condition ourselves (and those we lead) to be physically courageous like Benaiah, whether it be in sports and feats of daring at a young age, or in overcoming obstacles that truly challenge our greatest fears, or in dark and dangerous places around the world (and at home) where we must physically press past fear to do the right thing on behalf of others.

Such physical courage is absolutely critical and essential for each of us as physical warriors in the military and beyond. The reality, however, is that few of us (even those in military service) will be required to risk or sacrifice our lives to charge an enemy machine gun nest or defend our family against an armed intruder. If such a defining moment comes our way, may we be found physically brave and resolute, like Benaiah, Corporal Rudy Hernandez, Todd Beamer, and so many other brave warriors across the annals of history.

For most of us, however, our more frequent "Call to Courage," our most frequent challenge to "look fear in the face," will occur in the other domains of Comprehensive Personal Fitness™ introduced in *Resilient Warriors*: Mental, Spiritual, Emotional, and Relational.

Mental Courage

- <u>Fear of intellectually honesty</u> with self or others to examine facts and perspectives, regardless of where they lead. Speculations and anxiety about negative outcomes in the future. (MENTAL)

The need for mental courage to face down the fear of intellectual honesty is all around us. In the simplest of terms, what about our own income tax return? Do we let the numbers "fall where they may" and arrive at the right, although more painful, financial consequence? Or perhaps we are like a research scientist. Do we allow the data to "speak for itself," perhaps arriving at unpopular conclusions about global warming or other politically charged areas? Or, on an even bigger stage, maybe we can identify with high level business executives (perhaps in one of the high profile companies who have been exposed for corruption and greed), tempted to "go with the flow," underwriting deceptive accounting practices in order to keep the charade going. Each of us, in every walk of life, is tempted to cower in fear, to lie, to deceive when faced with facts that may work to our detriment. No doubt you have your own examples.

> <u>Each of us, in every walk of life, is tempted to cower in fear, to lie, to deceive when faced with facts that may work to our detriment</u>.

I remember many situations demanding mental courage and intellectual honesty in my own professional career in the military and beyond, one in particular:

"You must relieve that man today," shouted a very senior superior officer as I stood at attention. In Army terms, this meant I should remove this man from his position of responsibility as a leader, resulting in his personal disgrace and professional ruin. While sparing names and other details because of the sensitivity, this was definitely a "defining moment" for me personally and professionally. The subordinate commander who was on the "hot seat" had experienced a string of serious accidents and fatalities early in his command. This young commander was also slightly unconventional as a leader, not fitting the mold that my superior officer had in mind. Yet, I knew this young commander to also be one of the brightest and committed of any I had observed.

With significant trepidation and conviction, I replied "Sir, as I recall, you placed the guidon of command in my hands. I respect your experience and input, but I am still the commander. I do not think that 'taking this man out' is best for him, his unit, or the command. If you want him relieved, Sir... you will have to relieve me first."

While one has to be wise about "falling on one's sword" in such a way, we must be prepared for that time when we must take such a moral stand. Although it would have been much easier to submit to the senior's demand, I knew that it would be a cowardly decision based on pressure from the higher commander, rather than based on the specific facts of the situation. It would have been an expedient decision sending the wrong message through the entire command. While I recognized that the consequences for my refusal could terminate my own career, I also knew that it was not the right position to take. A section from the West Point Cadet Prayer, learned by heart in my early days as a plebe, echoed in my ears:

> "...Strengthen and increase our admiration for honest dealing and clean thinking, and suffer not our hatred of hypocrisy and pretence ever to diminish. Encourage us in our endeavor to live above the common level of life. Make us to choose THE HARDER RIGHT INSTEAD OF THE EASIER WRONG, and never to be content with a half truth when the whole can be won. ENDOW US WITH COURAGE that is born of loyalty to all that is noble and worthy, that scorns to compromise with vice and injustice and KNOWS NO FEAR WHEN TRUTH AND RIGHT ARE IN JEOPARDY..." (caps added)

As a footnote, this young leader to whom I gave another chance later became one of our finest senior leaders in the U.S. Army, leading tens of thousands under the toughest of conditions with the utmost selflessness, integrity, and courage.

The harder right instead of the easier wrong.

Spiritual Courage

- <u>Fear of moral and spiritual choices</u> that put you at odds with others and with the popular culture. Inward anxiety that if you dig deeply into your soul, you might come up "empty handed" (SPIRITUAL)

Resilient Warriors (pages 111-116) highlights the amazing story of Louis Zamperini, the Olympic athlete who forfeited fame to service in World War II. After being shot down as an Air Force crewmember, he found himself adrift at sea in a struggle for survival, then detained and sadistically tortured by his Japanese captors. One of his most profound acts of courage, however, was not on the battlefield. Rather, upon return to the home front, he struggled with alcohol and aimlessness until an encouraging wife and an irrefutable evangelist (Billy Graham) brought him to the threshold of perhaps his most courageous act of all: determining to surrender in faith to Jesus Christ.

This spiritual courage which overcame his fears of being vulnerable, admitting need, and swallowing pride led Louis Zamperini all the way home from his journey of purposelessness, negative behaviors, and fear. This is certainly representative of my personal faith journey, and that of so many others, which began with an act of spiritual courage to embrace a personal worldview which became life changing, but was seen as culturally unpopular or even unacceptable in some quarters.

As another example, there exists a distinct need for spiritual courage among senior leaders in our military and in our culture at large. In a day when the nation's military suicides are at historic highs and still rising, senior leaders need to exercise spiritual courage by ensuring the proper integration of faith and traditional religion into holistic solutions. Both statistically and anecdotally, faith and religiosity are very significant factors, particularly when addressing the wounds of the heart, soul, and spirit which afflict today's troops, families, and veterans. *Resilient Nations* (to be published in 2014) will address this need in more specific detail.

Emotional Courage

- <u>Fear of failure</u> and "not measuring up" to the expectations of self, others, or God. Danger of "being hurt" one more time. Apprehension about one's own emotional regulation, avoiding outbursts while conveying appropriate passion for a cause. (EMOTIONAL)

Emotional courage certainly overlaps with other forms of courage, but it largely consists of facing down the fear of not being accepted for taking unpopular stands. The leader who is strong and emotionally courageous will often champion important causes against significant odds, pushing through the emotional "downers" of criticism, glacial progress, reversals, discouragement, and fatigue or illness. History is replete with examples of social reformers who have demonstrated great emotional courage. Dietrich Bonhoffer modeled this as he diverged from the German Church as they became complicit with the illusions and depravity of Adolf Hitler. Such courage is well documented in Eric Metaxas' great book, *Bonhoffer*.

Similarly, William Wilberforce was the great social reformer in Britain in the early 1800's who was responsible for overturning the slave trade in the British Empire and beyond, as well as the reformation of manners and civility. We will talk more about Wilberforce in *Resilient Nations*, but for now will benefit from observing his emotional strength and courage. A telling excerpt from *Amazing Grace*, also by Eric Metaxas, makes the point:

> "Wilberforce was a tiny, frail man; for him, being brave entailed being very brave indeed. Once he was challenged to a duel by an unhinged slave-ship captain named Rolleston... the palpable stress of such a challenge and having to parry it in the public sphere must have been very difficult for Wilberforce. He knew that many people would say he was a coward, that this tiny, frail man was conveniently hiding behind his Christianity to escape defending his manhood in such a contest." (pages 163, 164, *Amazing Grace*, digital version)

As with William Wilberforce, emotional courage often takes the form of regulating anger and other emotions, even when your reputation might suffer or others criticize you.

Conversely, emotional courage at other times might be the right application of emotion to further a righteous cause. For instance, Christ was righteously indignant that temple money-changers were defaming his Father's holy place of worship. He boldly turned over the moneychanger's tables and forcefully cast them out of the temple:

> "12 And Jesus entered the temple and drove out all those who were buying and selling in the temple, and overturned the tables of the money changers and the seats of those who were selling doves. 13 And He said to them, "It is written, 'MY HOUSE SHALL BE CALLED A HOUSE OF PRAYER'; but you are making it a ROBBERS' DEN." (Matthew 21:12-13)

Later in this same chapter, the temple authorities confronted his actions:

> "23 When He entered the temple, the chief priests and the elders of the people came to Him while He was teaching, and said, "By what authority are You doing these things, and who gave You this authority?" 24 Jesus said to them, "I will also ask you one thing, which if you tell Me, I will also tell you by what authority I do these things. 25 The baptism of John was from what *source*, from heaven or from men?" And they *began* reasoning among themselves, saying, "If we say, 'From heaven,' He will say to us, 'Then why did you not believe him?' 26 But if we say, 'From men,' we fear the people; for they all regard John as a prophet." 27 And answering Jesus, they said, "We do not

know." He also said to them, "Neither will I tell you by what authority I do these things." (Matthew 21:23-27)

Jesus did not hang back when it came time to express righteous indignation on behalf of a noble cause. As well, He modeled emotional regulation and intellectual agility when confronted by angry authorities who were trying to trap and condemn Him. Again, we can do no better than follow His lead.

Emotional courage sometimes means showing emotion in front of others, even those you lead. While conventional wisdom suggests a leader should never show emotion in front of the troops, the reality is that genuinely expressed emotion messages true sympathy with the plight of others and identification with the victories of others, often gaining even deeper loyalty and commitment on behalf of followers. God gives each leader a certain emotional makeup, some being more expressive than others. I tend to be somewhat demonstrative, often expressing emotion (approval, affirmation, grief, sadness at the loss of others, etc.). As a young leader, I was often conflicted by this, assuming that it was detrimental for a leader to show any emotion.

In my early days as a battalion commander at Fort Carson (1-8 Infantry), I addressed the troops after a very demanding and successful field exercise. In the course of my post-exercise pep talk to the troops, I became emotional about our collective success and choked up for a few seconds. Collecting my emotions, I then finished the talk and went into the Battalion Headquarters. In my office I was momentarily "kicking myself" for choking up and "showing weakness" in front of the battalion. One of the young battalion staff officers suddenly knocked on the door, interrupting my moment of introspection:

"Sir, do you have a minute? I know you are new to the battalion and I wanted to pass something along. You may not know this, but George Pickett (famous for Pickett's Charge at Gettysburg) was a lieutenant in 1-8 Infantry in the Spanish-American war. He was a high-spirited type of leader who often cried when he talked to his troops. He also was uniquely able to motivate his troops to extreme acts of bravery. I just thought you'd like to know that, Sir. We don't see weakness when you show emotion. We see a commander that cares for us deeply and will lead us wisely."

This young staff officer had figured out emotion long before I had. I was grateful for his candor with his new battalion commander. After our encounter, I felt a new freedom to lead as God made me to lead, including the courageous and timely show of emotion.

As with all types of courage, there is a "ditch on both sides of the road." A complete vacuum of emotion or excessive displays of extreme emotionalism are not productive. Hence, the show of emotion must be kept in balance through exercise of judgment and wisdom, the focus of our next chapter.

Relational Courage

- <u>Fear of self-disclosure</u> with self, others, and God. Need to confront others or exercise "tough love." Insecurity about "not being accepted." (RELATIONAL)

In *When the Giant Lies Down,* Dick and Ruth Foth describe the importance of authentic relationships in order for leaders to exercise lasting power. Regarding what I would categorize as relational courage, they describe the importance of self-disclosure to the growth and relational health of a leader:

> "The snake sheds its skin for the sake of expansion. In the same way, we need to make room for emotional and spiritual (and I would add relational) growth. The key to that aspect of human development – and, indeed, any kind of meaningful relationship – <u>is the ability to self-disclose</u>. Self-revelation helps rid us of the tight-fitting prejudices that inhibit growth and separate us from one another. <u>Not to be able to be openhearted with another person</u> is an impairment to one's personal life that is immeasurable." (page 46, parenthetical comment and underlines added)

Dick Foth provides an exclamation point to this concept with the following:

"If 'know thyself' is a common and enduring axiom in the history of civilization, 'let yourself be known by another' has to be the other side of the coin. In fact, it's doubtful that I can know myself adequately or accurately without reflection from others." (page 48)

It takes relational courage for leaders, particularly senior leaders, to be authentic, candid, and ideally accountable to another person they consider a peer. For some, this is much tougher than the physical courage to face down an enemy machine gun. As I write this, I have just learned of the tragic suicide of a senior Army Colonel. He had breakfast with a close friend in whom he should have been able to confide close personal issues. When queried by this close friend, the Colonel stated he was "just fine," and then went home and put a shotgun to his head. While every such instance is complex, it is clear that this leader was emotionally and relationally isolated. His fear of self-disclosure, even to one of his closest friends, was apparently greater than his fear of death itself.

Yes, FEAR is a reality that leaders (and their followers) must deal with continuously. This fear strikes across every dimension of our being: Physical, Mental, Spiritual, Emotional, and Relational. If we are to truly overcome fear to "choose the harder right instead of the easier wrong," we must grow courage in each of these domains.

Choose the harder right instead of the easier wrong.

Gaining Altitude

Ecclesiastes 4:12 states: "And if one can overpower him who is alone, two can resist him. <u>A cord of three strands is not quickly torn apart</u>." (underline added) So it is with Selfless Service, Integrity, and Courage: the three primary strands of Character. This three strand cord of Character bears the loads placed on the shoulders of leaders: it does not break. These three strands, operating together in a leader's life, allow them to bend, but not break under the winds of adversity. This three strand cord is essential to resilient leadership: "Selfless Service over time from a platform of character and competence."

Let me close with a final story regarding deceased U.S. Army Lieutenant Colonel Boyd M. "Mac" Harris, a dynamic leader of character who possessed an equally dynamic faith. In 1983 when I was a student at the U.S. Army Command and General Staff College at Fort Leavenworth, Kansas, Mac Harris (also the brother-in-law of actor Gary Sinise) was a doctrine writer on the staff of the college, tasked with rewriting the Army's foundational leadership manual, FM 22-100. As a military leader informed by his Christian world view, he crafted a "Be-Know-Do" paradigm that placed renewed emphasis on Character (the "Be" component which is so uniquely and appropriately emphasized in the Bible) alongside knowledge ("Know") and action ("Do"). Although some might say that Mac Harris' primary contribution to the 1983 revision of FM 22-100 was tapping the powerful stories of historic "heroes" (such as Joshua Chamberlain, Commander of the 20th Maine at Little Round Top in the Battle of Gettysburg), his even more significant legacy was integrating Biblical truth focused on character into the leadership doctrine of the U.S. Army and beyond. The end result was a powerful leadership paradigm and foundational doctrine which still influences Army leaders today. Another end result, at least in a human sense, was that Mac Harris was diagnosed with late stage cancer during this leadership project. He died at age 39, leaving behind a powerful legacy in word and deed.

LTC Mac Harris' own demonstrated character during his military career and his life-ending battle with cancer became a powerful punctuation point to the relevance of "Be" (character, selfless service, integrity, and courage) in the "Be-Know-Do" equation which set an important leadership azimuth in the Army's post-Vietnam transformation. We are all richer for his sterling example.

Character does count, and these last two chapters are a fitting reminder regarding the importance of character, as well as the related "high core values" of selflessness, integrity, and courage. We now have other important ground to cover in *Resilient Leaders,* namely application of the Resilience Life Cycle© to leadership.

Reviewing our definition of resilient leadership:

"SELFLESS SERVICE

over time (implying RESILIENCE)

from a platform of CHARACTER and COMPETENCE."

In Chapter 4, we will conclude our focus on CHARACTER with a discussion of WISDOM, the critical quality which helps to balance and sustain the leader traits of selflessness, integrity, and courage.   In Chapter 5 and beyond, we walk through the Resilience Life Cycle© applied to leaders (Chapters 5-8). We will continue to address character and competence as we progress, holding them as tandem qualities for all resilient leaders.

Resilient Leader Takeaways

RL 19 – Not telling a lie is fundamental, but this is only the beginning of integrity.

RL 20 – Integrity on a higher plane is the seamless integration of faith, family, and profession into a God-honoring life message.

RL 21 – Our lives need full integration across the broad range of faith, family, and profession, but when a threat does arise, integrity also requires that we quickly identify the problem, seal off the broader impacts, and address the personal or corporate issue.

RL 22 – FAITH is the bridge which leads from FEAR to COURAGE, helping us to "hold on ten seconds longer."

RL 23 – Courage grows each time we stare down fear.

RL 24 – Courage is the cumulative result of staring down fear across the full spectrum of the physical, mental, spiritual, emotional, and relational domains.

RL 25 – Courage must be balanced with selflessness and integrity.

Additional Study

1. http://webweevers.com/integrity/ One of the most comprehensive and useful websites on INTEGRITY which I have encountered.

2. Foth, Dick, and Ruth Foth. When the Giant Lies Down. Wheaton, IL: Victor, 1995.

3. Carawan, Rolfe. *Profiles in Character*. Federal Way, WA: Lifematters Press, 1996.

4. Batterson, Mark. *In A Pit With A Lion On A Snowy Day*. Nashville, TN: Random House, 2006.

5. Conlon, Carter. *Fear Not*. Ventura, CA: Regal Books, 2012

4

Wisdom:
The Bridge between
Character and Competence

"'In our sleep, pain that cannot forget
Falls drop by drop upon the heart
and in our own despair, against our will, comes
WISDOM through the awful grace of God.'"
Robert F. Kennedy quoting Aeschylus
while delivering extemporaneous eulogy to
Martin Luther King, Jr.,
the evening of April 4, 1968, in Indianapolis, Indiana.

We have discussed Selflessness and Integrity and Courage. These are essential traits of character, yet, they are not sufficient.

WISDOM is the highly sought quality that bridges between character and competence, that moves us from theory to practice, that makes the difference between success and folly. The Bible succinctly states the value, and criticality, of WISDOM for resilient leaders: "The path of life leads upward for the wise." (Proverbs 15:24)

From *We Were Soldiers Once and Young,* there is a vignette worth a thousand words. You may recall the setting: 1st Battalion, 7th Cavalry, Ia Drang Valley, Vietnam, 1965. U.S. Forces were air assaulted into a small Landing Zone (LZ), soon finding they were outnumbered in a fight for their very existence. To this day, this Ia Drang battle is known as one of the most savage and significant of the Vietnam War. Only the courage and tenacity of the troops, along with great leadership in the fog of war prevented total annihilation.

I still remember the day in 1993 when then Lieutenant General Hal Moore, U.S. Army, Retired (the LTC battalion commander during the fight in 1965) and Joseph L. Galloway (a United Press International reporter, twenty-four years of age as he accompanied the 7th CAV into this fateful action) visited the 101st Airborne Division when I was Commander of the Rakkasans. This personal mentoring from a leader (and a reporter) who had "been there and done that" was a tremendous gift. As well, the detailed battle descriptions from their book have been invaluable; I still have the sketch notes from dissecting their book and teaching it to others over a number of years. Many have called *We Were Soldiers Once and Young* the most significant book of the Vietnam War.

An early section in the book describes Lieutenant Henry T. Herrick,

> "...red-haired, five foot ten, twenty-four years old, and the son of an astronomy professor at UCLA. He had joined the battalion in July and been given a rifle platoon; <u>he was a hard charger</u>.

> "I (referring to LTC Moore) mentioned Herrick to Sergeant Major Plumley and his response was forceful and swift: <u>Colonel, if you put Lieutenant Herrick in there he will get them all killed</u>.

> "Herrick's platoon sergeant, Carl Palmer, had voiced his own reservations about the lieutenant to Captain Herren after one of his men was drowned in a river crossing while on patrol. Sergeant Palmer took me aside after the drowning incident and told me that <u>Herrick would get them all killed with his aggressiveness</u>."
> (Moore, Galloway, p 68, parenthetical comment and underlines added)

That is basically what happened. In the early minutes of contact with the enemy, Lieutenant Herrick's aggressiveness and raw courage, combined with a lack of wisdom and judgment, led to disastrous consequences for his platoon and so many others.

> "And no other single event would have a greater impact on the shape of battle than what

Lieutenant Henry Herrick was in the process of doing.

> "Says Sergeant Ernie Savage of Herrick's orders: 'He made a bad decision, and we knew at the time it was a bad decision. We were breaking contact with the rest of the company. We were supposed to come up on the flank of the 1st Platoon; in fact we were moving away from them. We lost contact with everybody.'"
> (Moore, Galloway, p 70)

Now to the specific point: WISDOM is necessary to balance other highly commendable qualities of character, particularly courage. Without wisdom, courage can easily turn to folly. Just ask an earlier group of 7th Cavalry troopers under the command of George Armstrong Custer at the Battle of the Little Big Horn in the Great Sioux War of 1876. Custer was admirably courageous and certainly flamboyant, but his leadership also led to the unnecessary defeat and annihilation of the majority of his unit by the Lakota, Northern Cheyenne, and Arapaho Indians he was pursuing. Custer was highly courageous, but not equally wise.

> Without wisdom, courage can easily turn to folly.

Lest we get carried away with this point, let's remember that WISDOM does not replace the need for traits like courage, aggressiveness, and audacity. It does, however, provide balance and judgment in the process. Confederate General Albert Sydney Johnston (after whom my junior high school in Houston, Texas, was named) was a wise commander, yet he was also bold and courageous, particularly at the Battle of Shiloh when he moved in front of fearful troops and commanded, "Follow Me," placing himself at great personal risk to inspire their efforts, winning the day. Courage, boldness, audacity, and creativity are kept in balance by the wise commander, avoiding the "ditch of excess" on both sides of the road.

Solomon's Request: "Give Me Now Wisdom"

In the Bible, a young Solomon, when faced with the challenge of leading the entire nation of Israel, was asked a profound question by God Himself:

"Ask what I should give you." (2 Chronicles 1:7)

After Solomon reflected thankfully on God's transition of the leadership "guidon" from his father King David to himself, Solomon answered the question posed:

"Give me now wisdom and knowledge, that I may go out and come in before this people, for who can rule this great people of Yours?" (2 Chronicles 1:10, underline added)

I find it pretty amazing that Solomon could have asked for and received anything... riches, fame, pleasure... yet he asked for <u>wisdom and knowledge</u> that would equip him to rule a great nation. In response to Solomon's humble and selfless request, God gave Solomon wisdom and much more:

> "...Because you had this in mind, and did not ask for riches, wealth or honor, or the life of those who hate you, nor have you even asked for long life, but you have asked for yourself wisdom and knowledge that you may rule My people over whom I have made you king, <u>wisdom and knowledge have been granted to you. And I will give you riches and wealth and honor, such as none of the kings who were before you has possessed nor those who will come after you.</u>"

History records this is exactly what happened.

So it is with each of us. May we not pursue the fleeting trappings of leadership, but may we pursue wisdom and knowledge for the benefit of those we lead.

> May we not pursue the fleeting trappings of leadership,
> but may we pursue wisdom and knowledge
> for the benefit of those we lead.

Defining Wisdom

Merriam-Webster's dictionary defines wisdom as "a wise attitude, belief, or course of action... not imprudent or indiscrete... related to discernment, insight, perception."

The Scriptures provide an even clearer understanding of the value and meaning of wisdom: (underlines added)

> "... the acquisition of <u>wisdom</u> is <u>above that of pearls</u>." (Job 28:18)

> "...<u>in the hidden part</u> You will make me know <u>wisdom</u>." (Psalm 51:6, King David seeking to rebalance his life after a foolish and unwise tryst with Bathsheba and the related cycle of sin which included the murder of her husband in an effort to hide the offense)

> "...<u>teach us to number our days</u>, that we may present to You <u>a heart of wisdom</u>." (Psalm 90:12, a more circumspect King David who recognizes the leader's need to have a "heart of wisdom")

Although there are many other Biblical references to wisdom, I conclude this section by bridging wisdom to faith (parenthetical comments and underlines added):

> "The <u>fear of the Lord</u> (FAITH) is the <u>beginning of wisdom</u>." (Psalm 111:10), and

"But <u>if any of you lacks wisdom</u>, let him ask of God (PRAYER), who gives to all generously and without reproach, and it will be given to him. But <u>he must ask in faith without any doubting</u>, for the one who doubts is like the surf of the sea, driven and tossed by the wind." (James 1:5-6, underline emphasis added)

Just as Solomon, long before the time of Christ, we 21st Century leaders need equal wisdom to lead ourselves, our families, our troops, our professions, and our nation. May it be so; may we ask in faith.

Wise Leaders Make Good Decisions

Leaders make decisions. Wise leaders make good decisions.

> A divine **decision** is in the lips of the king (leader);
> His mouth should not err in judgment.
> (Proverbs 16:10) (parenthetical emphasis added)

In simplest terms, every decision a leader faces is comprised of the following sequential elements (although there may be multiple iterations through this sequence):

WHY?
<u>Why</u> is a decision needed? Why do <u>I</u> need to make the decision?

WHAT? WHEN?

<u>What</u> are our options? What if we do nothing? What are the second and third order implications of our decision? What are we missing?

<u>When</u> does the decision need to be made? When do we have enough information?

WHO? HOW?

<u>Who</u> are the key stakeholders in this decision? Who will execute and monitor the decision? Who else needs to know?

<u>How </u>do we implement our decision? How do we monitor the results?

From these key decision making questions, we will highlight aspects of leader wisdom which most contribute to good decisions and reduce the likelihood of bad outcomes, recognizing that good decisions sometimes result in bad outcomes despite the best efforts of the leader.

Wise Leaders Carefully Weigh Their Options

Let's dive deeper into WHAT. Assuming you have identified the need for a decision, a primary consideration is "WHAT are the available options?" In military parlance, what are our possible "courses of action?" (COAs) These COAs are the focal point of what the military would call the "Military Decision Making Process (MDMP)," as reflected in Army Field Manual (FM) 101-5, page 5-3:

Step 1. Receipt of Mission

Step 2. Mission Analysis

Step 3. Course of Action Development

Step 4. Course of Action Analysis

Step 5. Course of Action Comparison

Step 6. Course of Action Approval

Step 7. Orders Production

While this MDMP process is designed for use in complex environments involving hundreds, thousands, or tens of thousands of participants and moving parts, the general MDMP framework is useful for any type of decision. Basically, what are our options? Which one (or combination of options) is best? How do we implement the selected option, while minimizing the downside (risk) of the decision?

The MDMP process synchronizes the planning effort of many staff advisers, aligning with the Biblical admonition, "Without consultation, plans are frustrated, But with many counselors they succeed." (Proverbs 15:22, underline and parenthetical emphasis added). For the Christian leader, this "wisdom of many counselors" is multiplied many times over as we ask in faith for wisdom from the ultimate Counselor, God's Holy Spirit.

Sometimes the leader's intuition, experience, and this "wisdom from above" will cause him to favor a course of action which is not recommended by others. In this case, the wise leader must make a courageous decision with the corresponding integrity to take full responsibility for the outcome. Certainly, General Dwight Eisenhower demonstrated this courage and integrity when he prepared an alternative D-Day statement should the Normandy invasion on June 6, 1944 fail. His short draft statement read:

> "Our landings in the Cherbourg-Havre area have failed to gain a satisfactory foothold and I have withdrawn the troops. My decision to attack at this time and place was based upon the best information available. The troops, the air and the Navy did all that Bravery and devotion to duty could do. <u>If any blame or fault attaches to the attempt it is mine alone.</u>" (underline emphasis added)

As we carefully weigh our options as leaders, and render wise decisions, may each of us demonstrate the same courage and integrity as demonstrated by General Eisenhower.

Wise Leaders Learn and Grow in Wisdom for a Lifetime

Ideally we as leaders will avoid many challenging situations by learning from the wisdom (and mistakes) of others. To do this requires a personal commitment to a lifetime of learning.

In a nutshell, here are some basics that I have found useful:

- <u>Reading</u> is a critical element of growth. I know of a scant few successful leaders who are not avid readers. I think it far more important to read one book three times than three books one time. Digesting, analyzing, reflecting, and integrating with other bodies of information leads to mature thought and wise application. In *Spiritual Leadership* Oswald Sanders says it well: "The man who desires to grow spiritually and intellectually will be constantly at his books. The lawyer who desires to succeed in his profession must keep abreast of important cases and changes in the law. The medical practitioner must follow the constantly changing discoveries in his field. Even so the spiritual leader must master God's Word and its principles, and know as well what is going on in the minds of those who look to him for guidance. To achieve these ends, he must, hand in hand with his personal contacts, <u>engage in a selective course of reading</u>." (page 95, underlining added)

  I highly recommend the entire Chapter 12 of *Spiritual Leadership*, entitled "The Leader and His Reading."

- <u>Writing</u> (including active journaling, and perhaps blogging) and <u>Speaking</u> are also important stimulants to growth, forcing a crispness of thought and expression which serve to consolidate one's viewpoints and knowledge on a given subject. In addition to the growth potential that comes with writing and speaking, these are also critical competencies for leaders. You may have been a born writer or speaker, but I can well remember my early days of "fear and trembling" when asked to speak to a group of any size. Study and practice can transform both speaking and writing from arduous and fearful tasks into powerful and fulfilling tools for leaders to inspire and direct others. Lifetime learners will continue to hone their writing and speaking skills for their entire lives.

- <u>Teaching</u> others is a powerful way to "master" subjects, leading to lifetime retention. Perhaps you have heard that "the teacher always learns the most." I know this to be true. For military professionals, the first professional experience as an instructor usually leads to greater confidence, vastly improved ability to speak and think on your feet, and increased subject matter expertise which pays dividends in future roles. This certainly proved true as a result of my first instructor duty in the Engineering Department at West Point. Lifetime learners will seek opportunities to teach, whether in the military or in other professions.

- <u>Learning and growing from mentors</u> is also an important catalyst to consistency and accelerated growth and learning. An example from the life of General Dwight Eisenhower is instructive. Referring to a young Eisenhower just graduated from West Point, the Dwight David Eisenhower Memorial Commission highlights the pivotal time of learning which transformed this leader and equipped him for far greater responsibilities:

  "By graduation in 1915, the future supreme commander of allied armies was known to his classmates as a fun-loving maverick, one who had earned little in the way of academic distinction or knowledge of military science. Four years of schooling above the Hudson River had yet to shape Ike into a military leader.

  "Indeed, after several years in the service, Eisenhower was downright discouraged. Despite enormous personal effort, he had not been sent overseas during World War I, the 'Great War.' Then, when his intellectual potential began to emerge, he was slapped down by his superiors. In 1920, he was given a stiff verbal reprimand for having published an article about the future of tank warfare, an article deemed provocative and heretical by the Army's chief of infantry. Less than a year later he was stoutly reprimanded for an honest mistake that would have seemed trivial outside the Army.

"Without a combat record and having earned the disapproval of important superior officers, Ike's military future looked bleak. Then, in 1921, his three-year-old son, Doud Dwight, died of scarlet fever. Ike and Mamie were devastated. It was a depressed and deeply dejected Captain Eisenhower who took up his new assignment in January 1922 at Camp Gaillard, in the Panama Canal Zone.

"The Army commander at the Canal Zone, Brigadier General Fox Conner, had been General Pershing's Chief of Operations in France during the Great War. Wealthy, intellectual, and immensely respected through-out the Army, Conner had pulled some heavy strings to get Eisenhower transferred to Panama as his executive officer.

"For the next three years Fox Conner taught graduate courses in military history, strategy, and leadership in a 'virtual' classroom located in the humid jungle of Panama. This classroom contained a single student, Dwight David Eisenhower. Military history classes at West Point had been poorly taught. But Fox Conner stirred Ike's interest in history—he taught Ike how to read it, think it, and intelligently discuss its lessons. He drummed into Eisenhower his belief that another world war could not be escaped and that whenever it came it would have to be fought with allies. Having worked closely with British and French military leaders in World War I, he helped Ike understand that dealing with the enemy can be a simple and straightforward matter when contrasted to securing close cooperation with an ally.

"Eisenhower was transformed by his mentor. Three years of rigorous service and education with Fox Conner changed his life. Ike became a more serious reader of everything from military history to science, philosophy and the classics. With Conner's help, Eisenhower overcame depression and set out with determination to resurrect his military career."

This vignette illustrates the profound impact that a mentor can have upon the personal and professional future of a willing learner. While this is an example of a great military leader in the making, the principle applies across all domains of leadership and all categories of Comprehensive Personal Fitness™, including my own transformation at West Point under the spiritual tutelage of then Major Andy Seidel.

In addition to learning from the mentoring of others, we must also learn from our own mistakes. In the severest sense, we must learn and grow from the painful trial and tribulation in our own lives. We identified such growth as "Post Traumatic Growth" in *Resilient Warriors* (see pages 60-65), and also included a "Learn and Adapt" component in the Resilience Life Cycle© (see pages 190-195).

> ...in the severest sense, we must learn and grow from the painful trial and tribulation in our own lives.

Wise Leaders Invest in Others

Certainly General Fox Conner was a wise leader as he mentored a young Captain Dwight David Eisenhower, and other notables such as George Catlett Marshall and George S. Patton, Jr. His investment in these young, promising leaders literally changed the course of history. In like manner, each of us can be recipients of such tutelage, and we can also "pay forward" by wisely investing in others.

"Lieutenant Dees, I am selecting you to be my new aide. Your primary job this coming year is to learn. My job will be to make you a great company commander." (Brigadier General Tiger Honeycutt to Lieutenant Bob Dees)

As a wide-eyed infantry lieutenant, I had already heard many Tiger Honeycutt stories, and I would personally observe many more. I went into the job with fear and trepidation: what would it be like to work for this bigger-than-life legend, this leader who was known to devour Lieutenants and Captains for breakfast, Majors and Lieutenant Colonels for lunch, and conclude with a few Colonels for dinner? Imagine my surprise when this intimidating leader made it a priority to teach me how to command a company. And he held true to his word: "Bob, let me show you how that one happened" (explaining a helicopter crash); "Here's what live incoming looks like" (as we walked frightfully close to the bullets and artillery on a live fire exercise), and "This is the reason standards are important" (as we observed the tragic consequences of a leader shortcut which resulted in unnecessary tragedy). Sometimes the lessons and mentoring came without words, such as when we searched all night for a downed helicopter, eventually finding the two deceased crew members who had bled to death during our search: "Never leave behind a fallen comrade."

As a wise leader, Tiger Honeycutt recognized the importance of investing in others, allowing them to grow into their full potential as leaders and people. Sometimes his investment took the form of "tough love," and at other times it was as gentle as a nurturing mother (particularly when it involved families or pets). In a more humorous, but likewise revealing incident, Tiger really "locked my heels" (meaning to stand me at the military position of "Attention").

From my desk in the outer office, I suddenly heard Tiger bellowing, "Bob, get in here now!" This was not a good sign. I must have really messed up! Did someone die? Did I need to look for a new job?

Tiger continued: "Is it true that your bride (Kathleen) is at home with a sick puppy? And now the puppy is trapped under the washing machine?" (which Tiger had overheard in my distress call from Kathleen). "I can't believe you would let this happen. I thought I taught you better than this! Now go rescue that puppy now, Lieutenant." (...sort of like when your mother uses your middle name when you are in trouble.)

In a not so subtle way, he was teaching me that families, and puppies, matter. Ashamedly, I must admit that I did not intend to immediately rush to Kathleen's rescue, my initial reflex (albeit a bad one) when faced with something that would draw me away from my professional duties for Tiger. Thus was planted the seed which would culminate in the definition of integrity which we used in Chapter Three: "the seamless integration of faith, family (including wives, children and puppies), and profession into a seamless God-honoring life message." He was forging wisdom that would provide for the right balance of faith, family, and profession when the great challenges of leadership would come my way. I'll never forget the humor and the important lesson from that teachable moment with Tiger, who had chosen to invest in a young lieutenant.

One more example will be equally instructive.

"Pack your stuff, Major Dees. We are headed to the National Training Center tomorrow morning," directed Brigadier General Bill Crouch, the Assistant Division Commander of the 4th Infantry Division in October 1989 at Fort Carson, Colorado. Having arrived the day before as a battalion command designee, I had a few weeks to complete my in-processing and command orientations before the 1-8 Infantry change of command. Little did I know that my best battalion command preparation would take place on an impromptu visit to the sand, waddis, and dark nights of the National Training Center (NTC), under the tutelage of General Bill Crouch. Here again was a leader who chose to invest in a subordinate who had no expectation or right to receive such mentoring. Knowing that the National Training Center would be critical to my learning and success as a battalion commander, he gave me an invaluable "picture worth a thousand words." This immersion into the realities of tough, realistic Army training in a desert environment was literally a life saver.

As a final twist on investing in others, recall my story from Chapter 1 regarding the needless drowning of my former RTO (radio telephone operator), the ensuing investigation, and my final exoneration from any punishment for the mishap. Reflecting on the incident, I recognize that senior leadership could have easily ended my career, yet they extended "grace" to a young lieutenant who was still learning. Wise leaders invest in the future as they invest in the growth of others.

Wise leaders invest in the future as they invest in the growth of others.

Wise Leaders "Wait upon the Lord"

For those of you who have read *Resilient Warriors*, you will recall a story from my Army Ranger School experience (pages 98-100, *Resilient Warriors*). I'll briefly recount this incident and use it as a springboard for examining wise leadership further.

"'Okay, Ranger Dees: Our Chaplain is snowed out... you are it.'

"Thus began a teachable moment for a class of 300 future Army Rangers, stretched to their limits by lack of food, lack of sleep; and a grinding progression of night airborne jumps into the mountains of North Georgia, unending patrolling with a 100 pound rucksack, and runs on tender feet and wearied muscles.

"Little did I know that this was a 'teachable moment' for these Rangers and for young Army Lieutenant Bob Dees. Looking back now over many years of such teachable moments in my military, business, and ministry careers, I must observe that crisis truly does define the character of the leader, threat truly does clear a man's head, and leadership truly does make a difference.

The notion of 'not wasting a crisis' does in fact have validity for leaders who seek to help others navigate tough times and rise to a higher plane of performance. In this instance, the unexpected challenge to lead a bunch of tough, tired Rangers in worship became a 'cleverly disguised opportunity.'

"'Roger, Sir. Rangers, Listen up. God has a good word for us today. "Though youths grow weary and tired, and vigorous young

men stumble badly, Yet those who wait for the Lord will gain new strength; they will mount up with wings like eagles, they will run and not get tired, they will walk and not become weary."'"
(Isaiah 40:30-31)

Leaders become relevant when they provide wisdom, a "word in season" that speaks to the intersection of pathos, pain, puzzlement, and potential in other's lives, helping them surmount the challenges and complexities they face. For this group of Rangers, "mounting up with wings like eagles" was eerily close to the previous night's airborne operation, and the reference to running and walking was reminiscent of the daily reality for these young Infantry leaders who were at a new point of need and vulnerability in their physical, mental, emotional, and spiritual lives.

Let us look at this "word in season" out of Isaiah 40:30-31, with a particular eye to the different facets of a leader's wisdom.

A Wise Leader's Awareness of Inadequacy

"Though youths grow weary and tired..."

It is very empowering when leaders recognize they are inadequate for the task, allowing them to discard a façade of perfection and enabling their transparency as a leader. The reality and realization of inadequacy also point a leader to the living God who is adequate. *"Not that we are adequate in ourselves to consider anything as coming from ourselves, but our adequacy is from God..."* (II Corinthians 3:5)

Yes, youths... and counselors, ministers, teachers, parents, spouses, and leaders of all ages... do grow weary and tired, but the secret is to replace this human inadequacy with dependence on God who "does not become weary or tired." (Isaiah 40:28)

A Wise Leader's Sense of Timing

"They who wait upon the Lord..."

Waiting is a critical task for a leader. For Christian leaders, waiting upon the Lord is an even higher imperative. Yet, how long does one wait? When does waiting become procrastination or paralysis? In essence, this addresses the question of timing: timing of leader decisions and actions. Clearly, one seeks the golden mean between premature decisions with insufficient information and decisions which are late and impotent because one falls to the temptation of requiring perfect information before acting. So how do we do this? How do we "wait" in the right way and for the right length of time?

Here are some suggestions:

- <u>Assess available information to gauge when the decision needs to be made</u>. *"Count the cost before building the house."* (Luke 14:28) *"Know the status of your flocks."*

(Proverbs 27:23) Or I Chronicles 12:32, which highlights that the men of Issachar *"understood the times, and knew the way Israel should go."* We all do well to gather and assess the information critical to the timing and direction of our decisions.

- Use the time of waiting to listen to God and others. *"Seek the wisdom of many counselors."* (Proverbs 11:14, 15:22) Have confidence that waiting can renew your strength, and the Holy Spirit can and will reveal creative alternatives. Just recently, such waiting (and listening) prevented me from making a career ending decision in someone's life, instead discerning a creative alternative that provided new hope and a positive way ahead. I suspect you may have had similar experiences.

- Foster an obedient spirit. *"Wait for the Lord, and keep His way, and He will exalt you to inherit the land..."* (Psalm 37:34)

- Invest in JOY while waiting. Worship the Lord with expectation and gladness. *"The joy of Lord is my strength"* (Nehemiah 8:10) is not just a nice sound bite, it really works; often providing the oil of gladness that truly does give strength and optimism, even in the direst of circumstances. While this may sound "un-Hooah" (the antithesis of the Army's expression "Hooah" which implies high speed, macho, bold and unafraid, et al) to hard core military leaders or senior executives or blue collar shop foremen, it is true, nevertheless. The wise leader recognizes the power of JOY to sustain and strengthen during the toughest of times.

It is useful to recognize that waiting is often not a voluntary act. In our microwave society, people (and leaders) seldom wait when they don't have to. Often, seasons of waiting are also seasons of uncertainty, seasons of physical and emotional weakness, or brokenness.

A primary role of leaders is to model how to wait in a productive and biblical manner, similar to the words of James 1:2-4: *"Consider it all joy, my brethren, when you encounter various trials* (challenges, uncertainties, difficult decisions, seasons of waiting), *knowing that the testing of your faith produces endurance"* (strength, ability to physically and emotionally persist over time, patience to wait productively). (parentheses added)

As a final note regarding a leader's sense of timing, *The Gambler*, an iconic song made popular by Kenny Rogers, possesses a fair amount of leadership wisdom. In essence, it highlights the importance of the "when" and "what" aspects of decision making:

> "You got to know <u>when to hold 'em</u>, know <u>when to fold 'em</u>,
>
> Know <u>when to walk away</u> and know <u>when to run</u>.
>
> You never count your money when you're sittin' at the table.
>
> There'll be time enough for countin' when the dealin's done."

A later stanza reiterates the critical decision for every gambler, and serves as a metaphor for decision making in every domain:

"Now ev'ry gambler knows that <u>the secret to survivin'</u>

Is <u>knowin' what to throw away</u> and <u>knowing what to keep</u>."

The Gambler, written by Don Schlitz, ©Sony/ATV Music Publishing LLC, 1978.

The wise leader understands the importance of timing, and values growth in this critical competency, seeking to best know "when to hold 'em, and when to fold 'em."

A Wise Leader's Source of Strength

"...shall renew their strength..."

We have already mentioned the "joy of the Lord" and the "joy of knowing that trials are productive" as factors of renewed strength. As well, God's Creation and God's Word (as illumined by God's Holy Spirit) possess a spiritual and supernatural impact in the process of waiting:

- While I was an Army infantry officer who wandered through many a forest glade and rugged desert, I had plenty of opportunities to observe nature and marvel at God's creation. I also experienced such times of awe during recreation and reflection in God's outdoor sanctuary. Inexplicable in the human sense, "being with and in" God's Creation inherently renews one's strength, like an invisible battery charger. This is true in both "minute vacations" to dispel the stresses of the day, as well as extended periods of "soaking" in the wonder of Creation; from the microscopic marvels of an ant farm to the macroscopic grandeur of the Grand Tetons. For many years I have found that "getting lost" in the wonder of God's Creation, however big or small, is a good way to temporarily "forget what is on your 'TO DO' list" (perhaps the best definition of relaxation that I know).

- In similar fashion, Holy-Spirit directed <u>soaking in God's Word</u> (vs. intentional, focused Bible study) is inherently restorative and strengthening. We discussed such Christian "best practices" at length in *Resilient Warriors*.

Some may consider the suggestions above overly simplistic, yet I would consider them profound. As one who has often "dipped deeply into the well of courage," I attest to the supernatural recuperative benefits of "waiting upon the Lord" to achieve physical, mental, emotional, and spiritual healing, hope, and strength. While physical fitness is best obtained through rigorous physical activity, spiritual fitness is often best achieved through purposeful inactivity. We will expand this discussion in Chapter 8, "Careful Your Well of Courage!"

A Wise Leader's Wellspring of Vision

"...mount up with wings as eagles..."

You have no doubt already noticed my use of the term "Gaining Altitude" to conclude each chapter of *Resilient Leaders*. With waiting, and with height, comes perspective. "Mounting up with wings as eagles" is a fitting metaphor for the need of leaders to "gain altitude" to achieve vision and broadened perspective. One of the best descriptions of this dynamic comes from an experienced Army aviation leader, Master Sergeant (Retired) Brad Pressley:

> "The view of our world is very different at different altitudes. In NOE (nap of the earth) flight, tree tops go zipping by, the danger level increases if we mix speed with proximity to obstacles and we MUST be more vigilant in our clearing of the air space. This is a very tiring type of flying. As you transition to 100-500 feet, the sense of speed begins to decrease, you have a slightly better awareness of what goes on around you, more reaction time, and now you can clearly recognize features below you. As you get up 10,000 feet and beyond, you see a whole different world, you can see the curvature of the earth, you can see the smog or cloud formations below you, the feeling of speed is not perceived unless one watches and believes in their instruments."

Brad continues with a warning that implies leaders should not remain "at altitude" so long that they are subject to pride or they fall out of touch with those they lead:

> "A word of caution though, at this altitude, a few things happen: we lose touch with what is below us, navigation via a map and terrain association becomes more of a challenge, and the feeling of pride or power can begin to creep in, due to this new perception of being above it all."

Waiting upon the Lord, as well as gaining altitude to broaden one's perspective to achieve such enabling vision, are critical leader competencies. How do <u>you</u> "gain altitude?" How do <u>you</u> help others "gain altitude?" We will discuss this more under "Vision" in Chapter 5.

A Wise Leader's Sense of Pace

"...run and not be weary... walk and not faint..."

Your mind may immediately turn to the admonition in II Corinthians 15:58: *"Grow not weary in well doing, knowing that your labor is not in vain."* If one is to do this, if one is to run and walk over a sustained time, they must recognize the relevance of PACE. Running connotes a fast pace, while walking alludes to a slower, more sustainable pace. Pace is critical: when does one sprint? There are times when this is appropriate. How does one "catch breath" after sprinting? When does one walk? Even walking under tough conditions (heavy load, diminished physical capabilities, dark mental outlook) can cause one to become fainthearted, or to actually faint.

How do we as leaders avoid such physical, emotional, mental, or spiritual burnout? We will also discuss this further in Chapter 8, "Careful Your Well of Courage!"—Leader Self-Care."

Gaining Altitude

Wise leaders value and seek to grow in the important leader competencies we have highlighted in this Chapter. Wise Leaders:

- Carefully Weigh Their Options
- Learn for a Lifetime
- Invest in Others
- Wait Upon the Lord (Isaiah 40:29-31)
  - Aware of Inadequacy
  - Sense of Timing
  - Source of Strength
  - Wellspring of Vision
  - Sense of Pace

In each case, the answer begins with God. The answer begins with "Wait upon the LORD, and HE WILL..." renew our strength, allow us to mount up with wings as eagles, allow us to run and not be weary, and allow us to walk and not faint. You and I can experience this in our lives as leaders as we truly wait upon Him.

Now we have completed our high core discussion of CHARACTER: Selflessness, Integrity, and Courage. We have also established WISDOM as the characteristic that balances all other character traits, helping us to operate "above the line" to our full potential. We likewise note that WISDOM is the balancing agent between Character and Competence, bridging us between the "BE" aspects of leadership and the "KNOW and DO" elements. While examples abound, Solomon is our primary Biblical role model for WISDOM.

Similarly, we have established individual GROWTH as essential for any leader. This growth allows the leader to grow in wisdom and knowledge, in character and competence, as his responsibilities increase and his world becomes more complex. The leader who fails to grow physically, mentally, spiritually, emotionally, and relationally will stagnate, growing bitter and not better, falling increasingly out of touch with those he leads and the environment in which he operates. Biblical examples of leaders who grew throughout their life of service abound: consider Joseph, or Paul, or Peter, or so many others.

From here forward, we reintroduce the Resilience Life Cycle©, this time applied to leadership. As a reminder, this model (*Resilient Warriors*, page 68) is shown below:

RESILIENCE LIFE CYCLE©

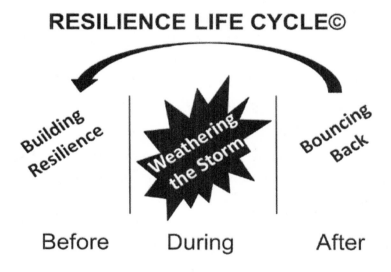

As another reminder, *Resilient Warriors* (page 200) expands the Resilience Life Cycle© to also depict the Before (6), During (5), and After (6) steps arrayed below each phase:

Before

- Know Your Calling (Mission, Purpose)

- Know Your Enemy

- Know Your Friends

- Know Your Equipment (Armor of God)

- Deploy with the Right Mindset

- Develop and Rehearse "Actions on Contact" (Get Ready!)

During

- Call 911 (Ask for help)

- Start the IV (Nurture yourself)

- Keep Breathing (Maintain routines)

- Draw from Your Well of Courage (Past strengths)

- Remember Your Calling

After

- Guard Your Primary Relationships

- Choose Forgiveness and Gratitude

- Grieve Well

- Sing a New Song

- Revalidate Your Calling (Discern and Chart the Future)

- Comfort Others

We will now walk through this model from a leader perspective, replacing the individual actions shown above with broader leader considerations. Chapters 5 and 6, respectively, will discuss BEFORE (Leading Before Crisis) and DURING (Leading During Crisis). Chapter 7 will dive into AFTER (Leading After Crisis), with Chapter 8 detailing the importance and techniques of Leader Self-Care. The concluding Chapter 9 shines light on the

ULTIMATE RESILIENT LEADER (Jesus) and provides a final challenge for each of us to follow His example as Resilient Leaders, serving selflessly over time from a platform of character and competence, making a difference in the lives of people, organizations, and nations.

Forward, March!

Resilient Leader Takeaways

RL 26 — WISDOM is necessary to balance other highly commendable qualities of character. For example, without wisdom, courage can easily turn to folly.

RL 27 — May we not pursue the fleeting trappings of leadership, but may we pursue wisdom and knowledge for the benefit of those we lead.

RL 28 — Wisdom positively influences the leader's decision making, growth, investment in others, awareness of inadequacy and vulnerability, sense of timing, clarity regarding sources of strength, ability to craft vision, and discernment regarding pace and capacity.

RL 29 — Wise leaders must exercise integrity to take full responsibility for the outcome of their decisions.

RL 30 — Wise leaders learn and grow for a lifetime.

RL 31 – Wise leaders mentor others, having a profound impact upon the personal and professional future of a willing learner.

RL 32 – The Bible is a storehouse of wisdom.

Additional Study

1. PROVERBS. Read one chapter of Proverbs daily to remind you of key truths and help you mine new nuggets of WISDOM. Given that there are 31 Chapters, read the Proverb chapter which corresponds to the day's date, and repeat the process each month.

2. Sanders, J. Oswald. *Spiritual Leadership*. Chicago, IL: Moody Bible Institute, 1967.

3. Armerding, Hudson T. *The Heart of Godly Leadership*. Wheaton, IL: Crossway Books, 1992.

5

Voice in the Dark!
Leading Before Crisis

I'll never forget high school football. There could be 10,000 fans in the stadium (football is big in Texas!), yet I could always hear my mother cheering. I could always hear her voice. What is that all about? No doubt you also have experienced this same dynamic in your life, whether it be in sports or some other endeavor. Miraculously, we are able to "hear the voice" of a parent, an encourager, a person who believes in us.

When I was commanding the U.S. Army's Second Infantry Division in Korea, I found that this concept of "voice" was very powerful. Our command included approximately 18,000 U.S. troops (along with many other United States-Republic of Korea coalition partners) located in 17 camps dispersed just south of the DMZ ("Demilitarized Zone") in South Korea. As I sought to impart the essence of leadership to our widely dispersed and complex formation, I recognized the need for a simple and effective way to communicate intent to our Division leaders. Our first "acid test" of leadership became:

"Do your soldiers know your voice in the dark?"

This simple question became a powerful military metaphor, referring to the specific practice of leaders who walk about in "the dark" to ensure their troops are safe, alert, and secure. This certainly occurs with young infantry leaders checking their soldiers in foxholes at night, but it also occurs in every other branch of the Army and in the other military services (where the "foxhole" is the aircraft flight line or the dark deck of a pitching ship or other military settings).

Although at the time I did not know the profound impact this simple question would have, it has become oft-used by military leaders and chaplains, as well as in many non-military applications: Do your shop floor workers know your voice in the dark? Or your children as you tuck them in at bedtime? Or your marital partner? Or a dear friend who has just suffered a life trauma? Or (fill in the blank)?

...we are able to "hear the voice" of a parent, an encourager, a person who believes in us.

The essence of "voice in the dark" is that if leaders are with their troops in the dark, they are sharing risk, they are building bonds of trust and confidence, and they are modeling selfless leadership.

I suspect you recognize by now that "dark" represents far more than the dark of night. In a broader sense, we are also referring to the dark of danger, the dark of despair, the dark of difficult challenges. If "your soldiers" (whoever that represents in your context) "know your voice in the dark," then they are also willing to trust you during their vulnerable times of fear and doubt. Such a relationship of trust between leader and led is essential.

Many people have asked me where "Voice in the Dark" came from. The simple answer is Jesus. Yes, as a military leader, I found Jesus to be my best leadership role model. I found the Bible to be the world's best leadership manual, conveying practical and powerful leadership principles for every walk of life. Specifically this principle comes from John 10, with Christ speaking as the Great Shepherd:

> "To him the doorkeeper opens, and <u>the sheep hear his voice</u>, and <u>he calls his own sheep by name and leads them out</u>. When he puts forth all his own, he goes ahead of them, and <u>the sheep follow him because they know his voice</u>. A stranger they simply will not follow, but will flee from him, because <u>they do not know the voice of strangers</u>." (John 10:3-5, underlines added)

Note that the sheep would not hear the shepherd leader's voice if he were not in the midst of uncertainty, fear, and trauma with them. Later verse 11 states the full magnitude of such commitment by the leader to share hardship with his troops: "...the good shepherd lays down his life for the sheep." (John 10:11) Sound like Selfless Service? I guess so!

Note also that the good shepherd calls them by name, the mark of a good leader who "knows his troops." Note that the sheep follow <u>because</u> they know his voice, a "conditioned reflex" that the leader has created by speaking wisdom, affirmation, and courage to his followers in past experiences. Note also that the sheep do not know the voice of strangers. In a leadership context, what a tragedy if we are a "stranger" to those we lead. What a tragedy if our voiceless (or misguided) leadership allows our people to perish. (Consult the negative (and evil) leadership of King Zedekiah in Jeremiah 52 for a Biblical example, or reflect on more contemporary examples in your own experience.) Or worse yet, what if our own voice is one of despair, discouragement, and damnation? May it never be so!

> In a leadership context, what a tragedy if we are a "stranger" to those we lead.

The Warrior David knew all about "voice in the dark." A particular example of this is in Psalm 29. He says, *"Ascribe to the Lord the glory due His Name; worship the Lord in Holy array"*, and then he goes into a series of eight verses where he talks about the voice of the Lord. He says, *"The voice of the Lord is upon the water"*, and a bit later, *"The voice of the Lord is powerful, majestic"*, *"The voice of the Lord breaks cedars"* and then a little further down, *"The voice of the Lord shakes the wilderness"*, *The voice of the Lord makes the deer's to calf"*, and so forth. The point is that David, this great warrior, leader, man after God's own heart, had spent a lot of time thinking about the voice of the Lord. I think we can say with certainty that David knew the voice of the Lord in the dark. So it is with all of us as we crash through our packed schedules, sometimes mundane days and sometimes terror filled nights. We must be careful not to rush past burning bushes (referring to the life of Moses, when God provided a "teachable moment" through a burning bush in the desert, Exodus 3), and miss the "voice of the Lord." Likewise, we don't want our followers to miss our voice on the dark and rocky paths of life.

We will introduce other "Leading Like Jesus" vignettes in the pages of *Resilient Leaders*, but it is next important to explain this "Voice in the Dark" discussion in a broader context of "condition setting."

Condition Setting

General Jack Keane, U.S. Army (Retired) was one of the best trainers and teachers I encountered during my military career. When I was an infantry brigade commander (Rakkasan Brigade in the 101st Airborne Division [Air Assault]), then Major General Jack Keane was my division commander. Although I knew inherently from growing up in the Infantry that "an ounce of prevention was worth a pound of cure," I did not fully appreciate the concept of "condition setting" until my time with General Keane.

"Condition Setting" in an infantry context recognizes that soldiers are the most valuable commodity on the battlefield. This is the essence of the "BEFORE" phase of the Resilience Life Cycle©. A leader should do everything possible to "set the conditions" prior to putting his troops in harm's way. In essence, what "enablers" can be employed to maximize success of the mission and eliminate unnecessary casualties in the ranks? In a military context, examples of such enablers are quality intelligence, adequate logistics, reliable communications, properly positioned mobility and counter mobility assets, echelonment of fires (progressing from air support, to long range artillery, to short range artillery, to indirect fire weapons, to crew served weapons, and finally individual weapons), and other means before the commander commits troops directly to the fray.

While such a systemic approach is not always possible, it is critical to "set conditions" in any way possible to maximize potential for a successful mission and for troop safety. Even in a fast-flowing "movement to contact," or seemingly routine patrolling, or convoy execution across IED-laden roads, there are ways to "set conditions" ahead of time. In essence, it is a practical and a moral responsibility for leaders to do everything possible ahead of time to ensure the safety and success of their subordinates.

Understanding and applying "condition setting" is an important leader competency for military leaders, as well as leaders in any other walk of life. To broaden the examples to workplace, academic, or parenting "leadership" contexts, condition setting implies likewise doing everything possible to "set conditions" to allow those under your charge to reach their full potential. For instance, the responsible business owner understands the need to "set the conditions" for his assembly line workers to be successful by providing the requisite parts, training, and incentives for sustained productive performance. The wise teacher inherently recognizes the need to maximize student success through clear presentation of content, insightful feedback on performance, and tailored assistance for both deficient students and highly gifted ones. And most certainly, responsible parents never put their young teen behind the wheel of an automobile without ensuring they do everything parentally possible to ensure the right training, the right practice, and the requisite maturity to handle the increased responsibility and risk.

To close the loop regarding our "Voice in the Dark" discussion, this is simply a way to express intent regarding the relationship of trust and confidence that leaders ideally establish with their subordinates and peers long before they are thrown in the crucible of combat or other challenges. "Voice in the Dark" helps leaders "set the conditions" for future challenges they will tackle together with their team.

> ...it is a practical and a moral responsibility for leaders to do everything possible ahead of time to ensure the safety and success of their subordinates.

Jesus had it right: "My sheep know my voice."

Setting the Conditions for Leadership Success

General Dennis J. Reimer, U.S. Army, Retired, was also a wonderful teacher and mentor for young Bob Dees. On the fateful day in August 1998, I answered the phone to an unexpected message,

"The Chief would like to speak with you. Please Stand By..."

Then Chief of Staff of the Army Dennis Reimer came on the line to inform me of a command crisis in Korea.

"I need you on the ground in Korea in nine days as Commander, Second Infantry Division." (We will discuss this "adventure" in greater detail in Chapter 6)

Although this would become a defining moment for me, my relationship with General Reimer had begun much earlier.

When he was the Commander of 4th Infantry Division at Fort Carson, Colorado, then Major General Reimer had a profound impact on then Major (Promotable) Bob Dees, the incoming battalion commander for 1st Battalion 8th Infantry ("The Fighting Eagles, a historic infantry battalion in the 8th Infantry which dates back to 1838, participating in every American War since the Mexican War). Within a few short months, he observed the family bus accident (described earlier), as well as the serious loss of a secure device that had to be reported to the highest channels of national security (we'll discuss this "cleverly disguised opportunity" later).

It was a less than sterling start for the new commander of the Fighting Eagles, but General Reimer (and his two outstanding Assistant Division Commanders, Bill Crouch and Guy LaBoa) mentored and trained me during these challenges, allowing me the latitude to likewise mentor and train my unit to better manage risk, turn obstacles into opportunities, develop greater precision in the fundamentals of war fighting, and build intangible aspects of will and morale into the heads and hearts of our soldiers and their families. I'm sure he did not realize the profound impact his trust and confidence were having in the life of this young leader. In short, General Reimer underwrote the leadership of Bob Dees and the Fighting Eagles as we weathered these storms together, and he underwrote our missteps, recognizing that this is how you grow leaders and the units under them.

On a lighter note, General Reimer (and his wife, Mary Jo) also discovered that young Kathleen Dees had a servant's heart, and greatly valued her role as their Army Community Service volunteer coordinator. I often felt he could easily find someone to replace me, but Kathleen was "one of a kind."

Yes, General Reimer was a great leader and he had a great impact on me. That is what great leaders do.

Simplicity

More precisely, I would highlight two primary leadership lessons from General Reimer. The first was SIMPLICITY. Although war fighting is a very complex business requiring deep analysis and extensive calculations, he modeled simplicity in his inter-actions. Such simple and artful communication of profound and difficult concepts empowered necessary understanding and subsequent application of the concepts.

Jesus also modeled this principle of simplicity when He used simple parables (stories) as His primary means for conveying truths to others.

Supportive of such simplicity, Einstein said, "The essence of genius is simplicity." As well, he said "Three Rules of Work: Out of clutter find <u>simplicity</u>; From discord find <u>harmony</u>; In the middle of difficulty lies <u>opportunity</u>." Although I can't attest to his practical leadership experience, Albert Einstein's theoretical prowess extended far beyond physics into the arena of human leadership, including an appreciation for simplicity.

In a war fighting sense, this means reducing challenging tasks to "Pavlovian simplicity." This expression refers to Russian Nobel laureate Ivan Pavlov's experiments illustrating principles of conditioned response in dogs and humans. Pavlovian simplicity alludes to reflexive action which is conditioned through training, as well as breaking bad responses through a process called extinction. These reflexive actions set the conditions for proper execution under the most brutal circumstances of chaos and confusion.

A familiar Army term is "KISS" (which is normally understood as "Keep it simple, Stupid). I would argue that "KISS" should actually stand for "Keep it simple, SMART!"

Willie Mays was once asked why he was a great baseball player. Illustrating the power of simplicity, he stated, "They throw the ball, I hit it. They hit the ball, I catch it." So it is—hitting and catching, blocking and tackling, the fundamentals always win, particularly under the most demanding conditions of life and leadership. Simplicity is very important.

Napoleon was a world class leader who knew the power of simplicity. After crafting battle plans to govern the complex movements of sizeable armies of personnel and equipment, he would summon a typically junior officer with limited experience to review the orders and confirm that he could understand them. If this inexperienced Lieutenant could understand the orders, then presumably they were simple enough to be understood by everyone else. This Napoleonic practice became known as "The Fable of Napoleon's Lieutenant." Napoleon understood and practiced the principle of simplicity.

So did General Reimer. He modeled the critical leader competency of distilling the essence of a problem into understandable pieces. Although discussed in a war fighting context here, this principle of simplicity applies universally. How do we as leaders communicate complexity? Do we seek to impress or to achieve understanding? Does our articulation of vision and intent leave people with a positive and clear azimuth or leave them scratching their heads?

General Reimer's emphasis on SIMPLICITY leads directly to the next discussion. In explaining leadership, he usually referred to four simple, yet profound fundamentals. While some senior leaders would highlight <u>four hundred</u>, he had <u>four</u>. I have carried these with me as the "90% Solution" of leadership for over 25 years now, teaching them within my own organizations as well as to leaders in many other nations, most recently to chaplains and leaders in Liberia.

General Reimer's leadership fundamentals were Vision, Team, Reality, and Growth.

Vision

Many *Resilient Leader* readers are probably familiar with the Biblical axiom out of Proverbs 29:18: "Where there is no vision, <u>the people are unrestrained</u>, but happy is he that keeps the law." or in the King James Version, "Where there is no vision, <u>the people perish</u>: but he that keepeth the law, happy is he." This is certainly true, illustrating that without vision followers sink into the lowest common denominators of lawlessness, discontent, and self-destruction. The military axiom, "If you aim at nothing, you will surely hit it!" is just the beginning of the downward spiral which occurs without vision.

The absence of VISION is a serious deficiency in any organization, team, or individual. This absence steals motivation, direction, and unity. The presence of VISION is a powerful enabler. It is the leader's responsibility to craft and cast such vision, and to keep it before his team. It is a clear "condition setter."

Major General Daniel York, USAR, is an experienced leader who well integrates his foundations of faith in everything he does. In his book, *The Strong Leader's Hand*, Daniel York captures the importance of VISION well:

> "To reach a place of solid leadership, we must understand and embrace vision! Have you ever served a leader without vision? Who pops into your mind? Was serving that leader valuable and good for the organization? Have you ever served a visionary leader? Whose image comes to mind? How did this leader influence that organization?" (page 14)

This quote implies an equally important question for each of us. Am I also a leader of vision? It's not too late to become one!

A story related to me many years ago involves three brick layers working along the sidewalk edge of a new building project. A man passing by asked the first bricklayer, "What are you doing?" He responded, "I'm laying bricks." The passerby soon encountered the second brick layer, seemingly performing the same task. He asked the same question, "What are you doing?" The second bricklayer, with a little more resolution in his voice, replied, "I am building a wall." Finally, the man passing on the sidewalk encountered the third bricklayer and asked the same question. This third worker stood straight for a moment and replied with strong conviction, "I'm building a cathedral." It was the same task for all, yet this man clearly had the vision which would propel him onward, despite the reality that there were many long, hard days (and perhaps even calamities) ahead of him.

"I'm building a cathedral! A chicken in every pot! A man on the moon! A computer on every desktop!" — All are examples of powerful, simple, captivating dreams for the future. In each case, vision makes the difference between drudgery in the present and eager anticipation of the future. In each case, it took a leader to cast such vision, and to help the team make it a reality. Let's dive deeper.

Further Defining Vision

While there are many definitions for VISION, I define vision in the following manner:

> VISION is a clear <u>focus</u> upon a future <u>end state</u> that <u>propels self and others forward with expectation and perseverance</u>.

Let me expand upon the key elements in this definition.

I learned about FOCUS as a young boy in north Texas—in Amarillo to be exact. On hot, sunny summer days when young "Bobby" was getting underfoot in the house, my mom would send me out to play... with a magnifying glass. My greatest joy was to find one of the prevalent red ant hills in our backyard and put my skills to work. After stirring the ant bed, I would focus the rays of the sun through the magnifying glass onto the back of a very large, scurrying red ant. With precision and lethality reminiscent of a HELLFIRE missile (the laser guided and highly lethal missile fired off of attack helicopters and drones), the intense spot of focused energy would literally explode the unsuspecting victim. Now perhaps this might make some squeamish, but for an enterprising ten year old boy in Texas "it doesn't get any better!"

This "picture worth a thousand words" made an important summary impression on me that became a life lesson. In short, VISION is like the magnifying glass. It focuses individual and organizational energies, resources, talents to achieve the desired future end state. Ten-year-old boys with a magnifying glass do this well. So do great leaders.

Great leaders also spend considerable time ensuring that the vision is aimed at the right desired END STATE.

When I worked in the Pentagon as a Brigadier General in 1997, I was Vice J7 and later Acting J7 on the Joint Staff, overseeing joint doctrine, planning, and training exercises of the U.S. Armed Forces. During that time, General John Shalikashvili, Chairman of the Joint Chiefs of Staff, had chartered the development of a new vision for our nation's military forces. Known as Joint Vision 2010, it defined a military capability end state for the year 2010 that drove a focused development of joint military capability for several decades. As a rookie one star general, I was assigned as the JV2010 spokesman for the Pentagon, a role which afforded me "church mouse" positioning among the power brokers (three and four star generals and admirals) who deliberated endlessly regarding this seminal vision which would focus billions of dollars of military resources toward best accomplishment of national security for the United States, as well as our free world partners.

Although I garnered many leadership lessons from these intense and important days of JV2010 development, the seminal lesson was the imperative to well define the end state. The wise senior leaders I observed knew that their greatest contribution would be invested up front, assessing future threats, identifying capability shortfalls, determining how to articulate the desired end state, and wrestling with how to "sell the solution (vision)" years ahead of actual implementation. Defining end state well is hard work. It is an essential skill for visionary leaders.

Finally, we draw from our definition of vision that it PROPELS FORWARD: "Vision is a clear focus upon a future end state that propels self and others forward with expectation and perseverance."

The reason people perish without vision is that they lose track of the noble goals they are pursuing. Essentially, "WHY are they draining the swamp?" (referring to the expression "It is hard to remember your objective was to drain the swamp when you are up to your neck in alligators.") The vision must be sufficiently far on the horizon and sufficiently "God-sized" in order to capture the imagination, the enthusiasm, the high and noble expectations that people need to keep moving forward over time. This sense of expectation is more easily attained when team members feel they have been integral to developing the vision. In essence, the team that "owns the vision" can better maintain the momentum in order to achieve it. The wise visionary leader will often slow himself down to allow the team to discover the vision themselves and embrace it at an early stage in the process.

> ...the team that "owns the vision" can better maintain the momentum in order to achieve it. The wise visionary leader will often slow himself down to allow the team to discover the vision themselves and embrace it at an early stage in the process.

A second reason people perish without vision is that they simply get tired. As well as being a good cheerleader, the visionary leader must work hard to keep the vision in front of the team, using it as a tool to pull the organization into the future, rather than dragging them out of the past. Simple and consistent articulation of the vision by the leader gives followers continued energy and expectation. This requires leader patience, resisting "presentation fatigue" which causes the leader to change or jazz up the message out of their own boredom, not realizing that while they have stated the vision perhaps hundreds of times, any given team member may have only heard it once or twice from the leader. The leader who vacillates the vision to make it more intellectually challenging or interesting for himself will often blur the vision for others, confuse the desired end state, and erode the focus and team energy needed to achieve the vision over a period of years and often under opposition.

The Limits of Vision

We have already quoted the Bible verse, "Where there is no vision, the people perish." (Proverbs 29:18a KJV)

Now for a corollary from my experience in the military, business, and non-profit ministry:

"With <u>only</u> a vision, the people <u>also perish</u>."

Said in terms which most statisticians would recognize, Vision is "necessary, but not sufficient." Equally important is the competence of the leader and his team to identify practically how to operationalize the vision. What are the phases by which we will achieve the vision? What intermediate goals and objectives will help us maintain the right azimuth and priorities? What is the division of labor among team members and team capabilities that best accomplish these intermediate steps? How do we map resources to our implementation strategy, ensuring best use of available assets (time, money, personnel, marketing, focus, et al.)? All of these questions can be appropriately clustered into the topic of strategic planning, the means by which leaders and their teams turn visions into reality.

Without making this a primer on strategic planning, I refer you to an extremely valuable book on Vision, Values, Strategy, Learning Culture, and overall Leadership: *Hope Is Not A Method* by Former Army Chief of Staff General Gordon R. Sullivan and Michael V. Harper. Regarding the concept that vision is not sufficient, they offer the following:

> "Vision without follow-through is a sure recipe for failure. In too many cases, what President George Bush called "the vision thing" goes no farther than the boardroom wall or the inside cover of the annual report. Vision and values get you to the starting line; it takes a lot of hard work to go from there to the finish line. The hard work is focused by strategy." (*Hope Is Not A Method*, page 99)

Let's capture two key bottom lines about VISION before we move on to discuss the remaining elements of great leadership: team, reality, and growth.

- It is the leader's responsibility to guide his team in defining the desired future end state, and to articulate it to his team clearly, confidently, and consistently; thereby propelling himself and others forward with expectation and perseverance.
- An essential supporting competency is strategic planning. The leader must guide his team in operationalizing the vision by implementing supportive strategies and

intermediate objectives which move the team successfully toward the desired future.

Team

In his great book *They Call Me Coach*, John Wooden's very first statement is,

"Life Is A United Effort of Many."

Certainly this man, the recently deceased "Wizard of Westwood" (referring to his seven national basketball championships at UCLA in ten years), knew about how to form a winning team from a group of players with diverse backgrounds, strong personalities, and differing views of the future. In short, he was a wonderful leader who embraced the principle of team.

Similarly, *Hope Is Not A Method* (page 237) emphasizes the importance of team:

"Rule Five: Leadership is a Team Sport

"Effective leaders forge alliances and build teams. They break down walls, floors, and ceilings, distributing leadership throughout the extended organization. Team building empowers people with a sense of responsibility so that the momentum for growth and transformation originates throughout the organization, not just from the top; it is about unleashing the power of people."

This principle of team is also reinforced throughout the Bible. For example, Genesis 1:1 (the very first verse) states, "In the beginning God created the heavens and the earth." The Hebrew word for God in this verse is Elohim, a plural form which immediately posits that the Godhead is a "team," known doctrinally as the Trinity (Father, Son, and Holy Spirit). This is further reinforced in Genesis 1:26, "Then God said, 'Let Us make man in Our image.'" again referring to the teamwork among members of the Godhead.

We also see this principle well illustrated in the New Testament by the Apostle Paul. Applicable verses from 1 Corinthians 12:14-21 read as follows: (Note the parenthetical insertion of "team" at each use of the word "body.")

> "[14] For the body (team) is not one member, but many. [15] If the foot says, "Because I am not a hand, I am not *a part* of the body (team)," it is not for this reason any the less *a part* of the body (team). [16] And if the ear says, "Because I am not an eye, I am not *a part* of the body (team)," it is not for this reason any the less *a part* of the body (team). [17] If the whole body (team) were an eye, where would the hearing be? If the whole (team) were hearing, where would the sense of smell be?
>
> [18] But now God has placed the members, each one of them, in the body (team), just as He desired. [19] If

they were all one member, where would the body (team) be? [20] But now there are many members, but one body (team). [21] And the eye cannot say to the hand, "I have no need of you"; or again the head to the feet, "I have no need of you."

Summarizing the principles contained in this passage, we see:

- There is one team with many members (v. 14, 20)
- Team members have different functions which all bring value to the team (vv 15, 16)
- If all members were the same, the team would be less productive (vv 17, 19)
- The team leader's role is to place team members where they best contribute to the team's vision and mission (v. 18)
- Team members need each other (v. 21)

Tony Dungy is a wise man of faith, a winner of the Super Bowl as both a coach and a player, and an uncommon leader. In his book *UNCOMMON*, he highlights the value of teamwork through a story about his former coach and mentor, Chuck Noll.

"Chuck Noll, football Hall of Fame coach of the Pittsburgh Steelers from 1969 to 1991 and winner of four Super Bowls, gave me my start in the NFL, both as a player and later as a coach. Coach Noll had a great way of keeping everything in perspective on those legendary Steeler teams of the 1970s. He use to assure us both with words and by the way he treated us that every player was important ("We need every man on the roster to win"), but he also made it abundantly clear that no one was indispensable. We knew that if one of our star players was injured, we could still play well and still win. So even though we had many Hall of Fame players, our games were never about individual accomplishments. Teamwork was valued above all. It was not about "I" or "me" but about "us" and "we."" (*Uncommon*, pp 22, 23)

No doubt you have been on enough teams to know the validity of these team precepts. Whether one of John Wooden's championship basketball teams, or a Tony Dungy Super Bowl team, or a family, or a high performing special operations unit, or a shift of factory workers, or the Church, we see that teamwork is essential. Great leaders understand this.

Earlier in our discussion of "condition setting" I mentioned the <u>"Do your soldiers know your voice in the dark</u>?" acid test which I gave to my leaders in Korea. A second acid test I provided was the flip side of this question:

"Do you know your soldiers?"

More generically, to apply to all the armed forces, we can say, "Do you know your troops?" This is clearly a principle we have heard before. Do you know your troops, or your teenagers, or the people on your shop floor? Do you and I really know them? Do we know their hopes, dreams, aspirations, gifts, vulnerabilities, weaknesses, challenges and their pain? These are very important questions for a leader. "Knowing your troops" is a principle that

I found to be true over many years, in many different situations, as I am sure you have.

Jesus again models this principle for us.

Here is what I mean. Consider John 9 regarding a man born blind. Jesus put clay on the eyes of this blind man and told him to go wash in the Pool of Siloam, a very public spectacle as the man stumbled to the pool blind. He then washed the mud from his eyes and could see immediately, <u>instantaneously healed</u>. Neighborhood critics and Monday morning quarterbacks repeatedly asked the man and his parents how he gained his sight. After many different "interviews," this young man summarizes "...one thing I do know, that though I was blind, now I see." (John 9:25b)

Now contrast this powerful story in John 9 with another example recorded in Mark 8:22-26:

> [22] *And they came to Bethsaida. And they brought a blind man to Jesus and implored Him to touch him.* [23] <u>*Taking the blind man by the hand,*</u> *He* <u>*brought him out of the village;*</u> *and after spitting on his eyes and laying His hands on him,* <u>*He asked him,*</u> *"Do you see anything?"* [24] *And he looked up and said, "I see men,* <u>*for I see them like trees,*</u> *walking around."* [25] <u>*Then again He laid His hands on his*</u> <u>*eyes;*</u> *and he looked intently and was restored, and began to see everything clearly.* [26] *And* <u>*He sent him*</u> <u>*to his home,*</u> *saying, "Do not even enter the village."*

Why are these stories so different? In one case, the healing was instantaneous, in the view of many people, and accompanied by public debate and proclamation. Conversely, the other vignette was a gradual healing (multiple "treatments") in a private place (outside the city) and publicity was intentionally avoided. Assuming that Jesus could have performed these healings in any way He chose, why did He use different techniques for different people?

I came to the conclusion that it is about Jesus "knowing his troops." It is about Jesus understanding the importance of the bent, inclinations, personality, and characteristics of every person, the importance of treating each person uniquely. In addition to the overall purpose that God be glorified, Jesus knew that one person could handle the public exposure, while the other needed confidentiality and privacy, leading him to a quiet place. Jesus modeled this across many different scenarios during His time of leadership on earth, seeing each person as unique and valuable. He knew His troops, and they followed Him.

So it can and should be with us. Each person is different and unique. When we "know our troops," we are able to bring out the unique potential of each person, resulting in the best for them and for the organization overall. We know this to be true as we have labored under leaders who only saw us as "a number on the roster," versus when we have flourished under leaders who truly knew us, believed in us, and brought out the best in us.

Leaders who truly understand "Team" know that they must appreciate the unique value of each team member. They must "know their troops," and their troops and the team will reciprocate in full.

Reality

"Bang, Bang, you're dead!"

"No, I'm not, you missed me!"

If you were ever a fledgling warrior as a young boy (or girl), you no doubt spoke or heard these words many times. My boyhood friend, Larry Day, and I spent hours pointing "bang bang" sticks at one another in mock war games. Cops and Robbers. Cowboys and Indians. Shooting at one another. Trying to determine who wins, who lives, who dies? All based on subjective assessments of hit or miss. While the implications are somewhat minor in the world of child's play, relying on highly subjective ways to assess reality has far greater negative impacts in the real world of families, business, or the military where dealing with reality prevents wishful thinking and tragic consequences.

Leaders must deal with facts, not fiction. It is important for leaders to value reality as a friend.

Equally dangerous is the leader who simply doesn't want to deal with reality or hear bad news. One of my early battalion commanders briefed me as his new adjutant with the simple admonition: "Bad news never gets better." He was essentially reminding me that he wanted to know the cold, hard facts when something bad occurred. He wanted to deal with reality. He was also inferring that he would not "shoot the messenger" that brought bad news to his attention. This commander was a wise leader who created an organizational culture which valued reality. Conversely, leaders who don't want to hear bad news are condemning themselves to a fantasy world where failure to deal with reality only defers and magnifies the eventual consequences.

Another wise leader, Abraham Lincoln, certainly had to deal with reality as U.S. President during a long, bloody Civil War. In his common sense manner, he reinforced that objective truth is not subject to interpretation. Perhaps you've heard a quote often attributed to Lincoln, "How many legs does a dog have if you call the tail a leg? Four. Calling a tail a leg doesn't make it a leg."

The post-Vietnam Army was characterized by a culture where many would "call a tail a leg" to save face, to magnify performance results, or simply from ignorance, lacking the assessment tools to objectively assess outcomes. While the transformation of the post-Vietnam Army into the magnificent Army of Desert Storm and beyond was the result of genius on the part of a succession of visionary Army senior leaders, there was one technological innovation that made dealing with reality a necessity, and eventually a virtue.

The technology was the laser. Adapting lasers to Army weapons (rifles, machine guns, etc.) and eventually weapons systems (such as tanks, helicopters, etc.), the Multiple Integrated Laser Engagement System (MILES) took Army training from "Bang Bang, you're dead" to an objective assessment which was irrefutable. Either your buzzer (set off by an enemy laser hitting one of your MILES harness or helmet sensors) was blaring in your ears, or it was not. Reality. Either your vehicle yellow light or your opponent's light (keyed again to laser sensors) was blinking, or it was not. Reality. Objective Truth. Goodness.

The impact of this shift from subjective to objective assessment of performance outcomes was profound, eventually resulting in a very healthy learning culture that exists to this day. With the laser, which allowed objective measurement of clear standards of performance, the discussion was no longer whether you were hit, because you demonstrably were. The discussion, rather, turned to more important questions such as: Why did I get hit? What could I have done to not get hit? What could I have done to hit the other guy? How should I modify my future actions to achieve a better outcome? Reality truly did become the friend of the U.S. Army. Many soldiers over the past thirty years owe their lives to the benefits of realistic training under realistic conditions.

Getting personal for each of us as warriors, parents, educators, business professionals, community caregivers, and leaders in every marketplace of life, how do you (how do I) deal with reality? Is it our friend? Do we encourage "truth telling" in our organization, or do we "shoot the bearers of bad tidings?" What do we do with bad news? Do we learn from it? Have we inculcated a learning culture into our teams so they understand the right ways to assess performance and get better? Have we figured out how to measure reality so we know when we have not met standards of performance, or so we know when preemptive action is required?

We will wrestle further with some of these questions when we get into Chapter 6, "In Extremis Leadership."

For now, we transition logically from REALITY to GROWTH, the outcome of proper responses to reality.

> It is important for leaders to deal with facts, not fiction.
> It is important for leaders to value reality as a friend.
> Leaders who don't want to hear bad news are condemning themselves to a fantasy world where failure to deal with reality only defers and magnifies the eventual consequences.

Growth

Chapter 4 stressed the importance of a leader's personal growth. As well, I refer you back to the pages of *Resilient Warriors* where we discussed the importance of posttraumatic growth (PTG) following trauma, as well as the overall necessity to continue to grow in our personal lives. You may remember the quote from retired Air Force General and Doctor, Jerry White: "As we grow older, if we are growing spiritually, we grow in hope. If we do not continue to grow spiritually, we grow in bitterness." (*Resilient Warriors*, page 65) This maxim in the spiritual sense is also true in every other arena of Comprehensive Fitness™ (physical, mental, emotional, and relational). Growth is essential to us as individual resilient warriors, and as resilient leaders who must continue to grow ourselves and our organizations.

We now focus on the subject of organizational growth, the essence of General Reimer's fourth and last precept for leadership. Why is organizational growth important? How do we inculcate a learning (growing) culture in our organization?

Organizational growth is important for both tangible and intangible reasons. On the tangible side, growth leads to increased value for owners and investors (in a for-profit setting) or increased impact (in a not-for-profit setting). As well, growth is also a requirement when faced with new missions that require greater scale or additional functions. From an intangible perspective, growth often lends to an air of progress and momentum, countering a perception of organizational stagnation.

Given the merits of growth for an organization, there are also potential downsides. Growth which is motivated by a leader who simply wants to "look good" is often counterproductive. "Growth for growth's sake" leads to a diffusion of focus and clarity. Undisciplined growth often leads to something the military would call "mission creep." Growth can threaten the distinctive culture of an organization which initially led to success.

While working with Microsoft Corporation, I found it interesting to observe their efforts to maintain their innovative pioneering spirit while transitioning to the largest software provider in the world. The business strategy to "start small and scale fast" has merit, but scaling a solution is not easy. Often "quantity takes on a quality all its own," meaning that the greater quantities associated with growth sometimes inject <u>qualitative differences</u> which require substantively different approaches.

In this regard, I have learned that leaders who fail to adapt to larger scale are often trapped in "doing it the way we have always done it," only faster.   Such leaders, for instance, often have a difficult time transitioning from company to battalion to brigade to even higher command as a senior leader.   The leader with potential to be a senior leader must possess the adaptability to recognize that leading a battalion takes far more than simply leading a company five times over. This same principle holds true in other sectors as well.

As a momentary comic relief to this discussion of organizational growth, let me highlight the leader adaptability to which I have just referred.   At West Point, plebes sit at the end of the table opposite the Table Commandant and perform certain duties for the ten cadets at the table.   One of the duties is to cut desserts. The incentive for doing it well is that a plebe charged with dessert cutting will often lose their dessert if the task is not performed to standard. Plebes query the table to determine how many pieces of dessert to cut, then use a "dessert template" (carried in plastic in their hats) to ensure they can cut equally sized pieces of pie or cake. The responsible plebe always hopes for an even number of pieces, knowing his task will be far easier, and that he may actually get dessert for that meal.

The moment comes to cut the apple pie. Upon inquiring, our plebe learns he will need to cut seven pieces. Ouch! That is hard! After working diligently to perform the task, the plebe soon recognizes that he has botched the job. Oh no! Not to be undone, our enterprising plebe quickly scrambles the pie to the best of his ability and confidently announces, "Apple <u>cobbler</u> to the head of the table for inspection, Sir!" Although the incident is humorous, this plebe was definitely thinking on his feet, demonstrating an adaptability that has no doubt held him in good stead.

Given the tangible and intangible merits of organizational growth, as well as the potential downsides; let me provide some concluding observations:

- Leaders must <u>drive growth</u>, instead of letting growth drive them.
- To drive growth requires an <u>intentional strategy</u> (There's that word again!) which gauges the ability of the organization to absorb change and expansion while setting out the rationale and objectives for such growth.
- The purpose for growth must be <u>well articulated</u> to the team, and opposition to the associated changes should be identified and addressed.
- Leaders must stay alert to the <u>need for new methods</u>, new skills, and new perspectives required by growth.
- Leaders who espouse growth must provide their organization with the <u>resources</u> to accomplish it.
- Leaders seeking growth should be careful to mitigate negative impacts on their <u>organizational culture</u>.
- Increased risk scenarios often accompany growth, requiring <u>enhanced risk management processes</u>.

Growth is usually a good thing, but seldom easy or simple. Jesus' analogies regarding the high cost of discipleship also provide wise counsel for leaders navigating organizational growth:

> [28] *For which one of you, when he wants to build a tower* (grow), *does not first sit down and calculate the cost to see if he has enough to complete it?* (assess the impacts and required resources) [29] *Otherwise, when he has laid a foundation and is not able to finish, all who observe it begin to ridicule him* (impact on organizational reputation), [30] *saying, 'This man began to build and was not able to finish.'* [31] *Or what king, when he sets out to meet another king in battle* (take on a new mission), *will not first sit down and consider* (strategize) *whether he is strong enough with ten thousand men to encounter the one coming against him with twenty thousand?* (Luke 14:28-31, parenthetical comments added)

Gaining Altitude

So there you have it. Within the context of the Resilience Life Cycle©, this discussion has been about the "Before" phase. What actions does a leader take <u>before</u> the storm hits to "set the conditions" for success? While many other competencies could be discussed, I have put the spotlight on SIMPLICITY, VISION, TEAM, REALITY, and GROWTH.

By the way:

"Do your troops know your voice in the dark?"

"Do you know your troops?"

Now we continue our progression through the Resilience Life Cycle© shown below:

RESILIENCE LIFE CYCLE©

Before   During   After

Next up: Chapter 6, "Leading During Crisis."

Resilient Leader Takeaways

RL 33 – "Condition Setting," applicable across all arenas of life and leadership, is the leader's responsibility to do everything possible before a complex or dangerous mission to ensure successful accomplishment at a minimum of risk to personnel and other resources.

RL 34 – "Do your soldiers know your voice in the dark?" refers to setting the conditions of trust and confidence between leader and led.

RL 35 – "Do you know your troops?" is a condition setter which emphasizes the leader's appreciation of the unique strengths, weaknesses, and personal bent of those they lead.

RL 36 – Simplicity is a leader virtue, allowing communication of profound and difficult concepts which ensures necessary understanding and application.

RL 37 – Four essential leadership fundamentals are Vision, Team, Reality, and Growth.

RL 38 – VISION is a clear <u>focus</u> upon a future <u>end state</u> that <u>propels self and others forward with expectation and perseverance</u>.

RL 39 – Vision is essential, but not sufficient without practical strategies to operationalize the vision. Strategic planning is an essential supporting competency. The leader must guide his team in operationalizing the vision by implementing supportive strategies and intermediate objectives which move the team successfully toward the desired future.

RL 40 – TEAM is a group of <u>interdependent</u> players who exercise <u>uniquely valuable functions</u> towards the <u>accomplishment</u> of a <u>shared vision and mission</u>.

RL 41 – The leader is responsible for guiding his team in defining the desired future end state, and to articulate it to his team clearly, confidently, and consistently.

RL 42 – The team that "owns the vision" can better maintain momentum in order to achieve it. The wise visionary leader will often slow down to allow the team to discover the vision themselves and embrace it at an early stage in the process.

RL 43 – REALITY is important for leaders who need facts, not fiction. It is important for leaders to value reality as a friend. Leaders who avoid bad news are condemning themselves to a fantasy world where failure to deal with reality only defers and magnifies the eventual consequences.

RL 44 – GROWTH is an essential organizational goal that prevents stagnation, leads to new opportunities and approaches, and instills a quest for continuous improvement.

Additional Study

1. York, Daniel. *The Strong Leader's Hand.* Charleston, SC: First Cause, 2011.

2. Dungy, Tony. *Uncommon.* Winter Park, FL: Tyndale, 2009.

3. Townsend, John. *Leadership Beyond Reason.* Nashville, TN: Thomas Nelson, 2009.

4. Bossidy, Larry, and Charan, Ram. *Execution.* New York, NY: Random House, 2009.

5. Sullivan, Gordon R., and Harper, Michael V. *Hope Is Not A Method.* New York, NY: Random House, 1996.

6. Wooden, John. *They Call Me Coach.* With Jack Tobin. New York, NY: The McGraw-Hill Companies, 2004.

7. Gongwer, Todd G. *LEAD...for God's Sake!* Carol Stream, IL: Tyndale House Publishers, Inc., 2011.

6

Sir, We Have a Situation!
Leading During Crisis

"They came to Jesus and woke Him up, saying 'Master, Master,
we are perishing!'
And He got up and rebuked the wind and the surging waves,
and they stopped, and it became calm."
Luke 8:24

As the Ultimate Resilient Leader, Jesus provided calm in the storm for his frightened disciples. This is what good leaders do, making a positive difference for others in the storms of life, just as the Prophet Isaiah instructs in Isaiah 35:3-4:

"Encourage the exhausted, and strengthen the feeble. Say to those with anxious heart, 'Take courage, fear not...'"

The Apostle Paul demonstrates similar leadership in another storm at sea (Acts 27). After being castigated by Jewish leaders for speaking to the people about his conversion experience and teachings deemed contrary to the Jewish faith, Paul was placed under custody of the occupying Roman officials for resolution of the complaints against him. While testifying to local Roman officials, Paul "appealed to Caesar" as a Roman citizen, meaning that he would be transported to Rome for trial, somewhat similar to a case being referred to the Supreme Court. For the sea voyage to Rome, Paul was placed under the custody of a Roman officer named Julius. This journey across a stormy sea soon became "interesting," in fact, a full blown struggle between life and death, hope and despair (Acts 27:18-22, bold emphasis added):

"[18] The next day as we were being violently storm-tossed, they began to jettison the cargo; [19] and on the third day they threw the ship's tackle overboard with their own hands. [20] **Since neither sun nor stars appeared for many days, and no small storm was assailing us, from then on all hope of our being saved was gradually abandoned.** [21] When they had gone a long time without food, then Paul stood up in their midst and said, "Men, you ought to have followed my advice and not to have set sail from Crete and incurred this damage and loss. **²² Yet now I urge you to keep up your courage, for there will be no loss of life among you, but only of the ship."**

This crisis at sea continued for fourteen days until it culminated with an imminent shipwreck on rugged coastal rocks (Acts 27:30-38, bold emphasis added):

³⁰ But as the sailors were trying to escape from the ship and had let down the *ship's* boat into the sea, on the pretense of intending to lay out anchors from the bow, ³¹ Paul said to the centurion and to the soldiers, **"Unless these men remain in the ship, you yourselves cannot be saved."** ³² Then the soldiers cut away the ropes of the *ship's* boat and let it fall away.

³³ Until the day was about to dawn, **Paul was encouraging them** all to take some food, saying, "Today is the fourteenth day that you have been constantly watching and going without eating, having taken nothing. ³⁴ Therefore **I encourage you to take some food**, for this is for your preservation, **for not a hair from the head of any of you will perish."** ³⁵ Having said this, he took bread and **gave thanks to God** in the presence of all, and he broke it and began to eat. ³⁶ **All of them were encouraged** and they themselves also took food. ³⁷ All of us in the ship were two hundred and seventy-six persons. ³⁸ When they had eaten enough, they

began to lighten the ship by throwing out the wheat into the sea.

Ultimately, the ship was wrecked as it neared land, but all 276 on board were saved. In the course of this crisis, Paul conveyed calm confidence, provided encouragement, inserted moral clarity, and pointed those in dire circumstances to the God of Hope. This is what "in extremis" leaders do.

In his book *In Extremis Leadership*, Colonel Tom Kolditz provides another example of how a leader helps others "weather the storm." The setting is along the Demilitarized Zone (DMZ) in Korea. As an artillery battalion commander, Tom Kolditz was awakened late in the evening on Halloween 1998 to learn that one of his armored personnel carriers had erratically swerved on a bridge, broken through the concrete siding, plunged 90 feet into the Imjin River, and came to rest under 30-40 feet of water with five of his soldiers trapped inside (who eventually drowned). This was definitely an unfolding crisis of tragic human proportion as well as one with significant political and military implications. He records the early moments as he arrived at the scene of the accident:

> "As the helicopter flared to land near the bridge, I could see searchlights, medical evacuation helicopters, ambulances, soldiers moving about, and a few Koreans from a nearby village who were willing to leave their beds at 2:00 A.M. to witness the activity. As I walked across the bridge to the gaping hole in the concrete wall, I saw a camouflaged entourage of staff officers walking

to the same place. Centered in the throng was the Second Infantry Division commander, Major General Bob Dees. He was responsible for more than seventeen thousand soldiers, five of whom had drawn their last breath. I saluted, and we exchanged the greeting of the division: 'Second to none, Sir.' After rendering a report with the information I had, I looked him in the eye, took a deep breath, and sighed. An accident of this magnitude would be on CNN in an hour, and five families would soon open their doors on Halloween eve, candy in hand, to find a casualty notification officer and an Army chaplain on their step. It was unquestionably the lowest point in my life thus far.

"General Dees looked back at me and without hesitation said, 'You know, Tom, it's not whether bad things happen that makes or breaks a commander. It's what he does with the hand he's dealt that really matters.' His message was characteristic of a leader who had lost people in the past, and knew that more would be lost in the future. Leading is about respecting the dead and helping the organization grieve, not about how the leader feels. Death announces to good leaders that it's time to lead the living. Bob Dees is an in extremis leader." (*In Extremis Leadership*, pages 138,139)

Colonel Tom Kolditz also proved himself to be an in extremis leader as he led his team through crisis and forward to many future successes. I highly recommend his book for an in-depth examination of in extremis leadership.

Helping Others Weather the Storm

Given this preamble to in extremis leadership let me provide some key points of emphasis from my own experience. While there are many topics we could examine, I will focus on six "best practices" for helping others "weather the storm:"

- Positively Affirm Those in the Crucible

- Let the Experts do their job

- Seek Historical Parallels

- Shield Subordinates

- Lead by Example

- Mobilize Resources

> "...it's not whether bad things happen that makes or breaks a commander. It's what he does with the hand he's dealt that really matters."

Positively Affirm Those in the Crucible

As with the Kolditz vignette relayed earlier, a crisis is not the time to play "woulda, coulda, shoulda." Leaders must resist the inclination to imply "I told you so" or to find fault and assess blame. A crisis is not the time for an after action review critique; rather, it is the time for positive attitudes and actions to work the crisis to a best possible conclusion.

Conversely, leading others through crisis includes affirming subordinates personally, expressing confidence in their ability to lead through the crisis (assuming there has <u>not</u> been a significant breech of confidence or significant display of incompetence, which is usually the case), and providing broader perspective that "normalizes" the experience for the leader in the crucible of crisis (such as when I told Tom Kolditz, "You know, Tom, it's not whether bad things happen that makes or breaks a commander. It's what he does with the hand he's dealt, that really matters."). In essence, we as leaders need to "give life" to others navigating crisis, providing encouragement (putting courage in others) to press through the daunting circumstances.

Let the Experts Do Their Jobs

While teaching Patterns of Problem Solving at West Point in the 1980s, I recall a study which highlighted the role of leaders during major manmade disasters, such as nuclear power plant meltdowns, groundings of large ships, and aviation emergencies. The primary observation was that leaders often "got in the way" of the subject matter experts at exactly the wrong time, making the situation even worse. Left unhindered, these experts knew which buttons to push, which emergency procedures to follow, which actions to take to alleviate the crisis. Regrettably, heavy handed (and often insecure) leaders often inserted themselves and became "part of the problem rather than part of the solution," even in some cases precipitating preventable disasters.

For example, in the Kolditz scenario, it would have been totally counterproductive for me as the senior commander to start directing the search efforts of the Korean rescue divers or other actions being taken to rectify the situation. While the leader should not assume a totally passive approach in a crisis, they must know "when and how to stay out of the way," allowing the subordinates they have mentored and trained to do their jobs, particularly when facing a time sensitive crisis.

Seek Historical Parallels

As the senior leader "gains altitude" and considers creative solutions to the crisis, it is useful to consider historical parallels. When I reported into 1st Armored Division ("Old Ironsides") in Germany in 1984, I was assigned as the Division War Planner ("G3 Plans"). Very soon after my arrival, then Commanding General

Major General Crosbie E. Saint directed me to write a new GDP ("General Defense Plan") for the division. While not a crisis from Major General Saint's perspective, Major Dees saw it through a different lens. Never having been assigned to a mechanized or armored unit, I was now expected to write the war plan for an entire armored division, at the height of the Cold War in Europe. This was a big deal. Although there were a lot of talented people to assist with this critical project, I felt very inadequate for the task. Not to be overdramatic, but the situation represented a professional crisis in my world.

In the early phase of this GDP effort, I asked the question, "Who has been here before? This is historic ground, what warriors of decades or centuries before fought on this ground?" Some rudimentary research uncovered Napoleon's Jena-Auerstadt Campaign of 1806 in which a major mountain complex called the Fichtelgebirge in German Bavaria became a prominent determinant of the campaign. The lights went on, allowing us to use Napoleon's movements over the same terrain to provide creative insight regarding how to capitalize upon the same geography almost one hundred and seventy years later.

Searching for historical parallel is a powerful practice for leaders seeking creative ways to navigate complex challenges and crises. At the end of this chapter, I will relay a more substantive example as I assumed command of the Second Infantry Division in Korea under the clouds of crisis.

Shield Subordinates

Often the leader must serve as a "heat shield" for subordinates who are working the crisis. As highlighted early in Chapter 1, people who have been hurt and disillusioned by tragedy and crisis often want to strike out at the leaders in charge. While understandable, this dynamic can often be a significant distraction for those actually navigating the crisis. As well, the media is an ever present reality, with the degree of their involvement normally proportional to the "ugliness" of the situation.

In Chapter 1, I spoke of the bus rollover accident at Fort Carson and the need as a leader in crisis to absorb the slings and arrows of hurting people as well as deal with a curious press who were going to report the story, with or without the right information. Little did I know, but the lessons learned in that crisis helped me lead others through a similar storm in Korea a decade later. The Korean situation involved a suspected terrorist plot, specifically an intelligence report that alleged that a terrorist had placed a pipe bomb in a "mogas" railcar (mogas is a highly volatile fuel, similar to what one puts in a private automobile versus less volatile diesel fuel or aviation gas). The "blast effects" radius of such a scenario was not measured in feet, but miles, raising the potential of jeopardizing thousands of lives and placing significant US and South Korea property at risk. While we took steps to validate this threat, search for pipe bombs in over a hundred rail cars at the suspected location, and determine appropriate responses, I directed that we evacuate the closest Korean town in the middle of the night. This action made me most unpopular with the threatened and inconvenienced Korean civilians. While the crisis continued to unfold, their complaints reached the floor of the South Korean Congress the next morning, with legislators demanding a full investigation and perhaps a reprimand to the commander (me) who had directed such an evacuation. Needless to say, the political and public affairs aspects of this situation were starting to spin out of control.

Reflecting back on the Fort Carson bus rollover of a decade earlier, I called a press conference with Korean media to convey information regarding the serious nature of the threat and the necessity of the evacuation. This, along with helpful intervention by my higher headquarters, somewhat allayed the rising hostility of South Korea governmental leaders. As well, I had my Public Affairs Officer organize a town hall meeting for the displaced Korean civilians. Unknown to them, we also arranged for a community steak dinner with a final coup de grace, Second Infantry Division baseball caps for each of the Koreans. The town hall meeting allowed them to ventilate, while the follow on meal reinstituted good will with our host nation civilians.

These actions to shield my subordinates from much of the civilian and political fallout allowed them to work the problem, assessing and reducing the risk resulting from the terrorist threat.

Lead by Example

While "lead by example" is a basic leadership principle, it often becomes obvious in a crisis that the leader needs to demonstrate courage and initiative to break the paralysis that sometimes afflicts individuals and organizations in times of chaos and confusion. While the following is a somewhat humorous example, it nevertheless illustrates the point.

While on my first field exercise with 1-8 Infantry at Fort Carson, one of our attached armor soldiers lost a KY 38 encryption device, a very serious loss which required immediate reporting to the National Security Agency (NSA) within a matter of hours. As with the loss of any sensitive item (weapons, classified information, encryption devices, et al), Army policy and practice dictates that the losing unit continues to search for the sensitive item, often being quarantined until the item is found or unit higher headquarters calls off the search. Such searches can often extend to weeks, as I well know.

After the battalion spent almost a week of searching (instead of training!) for the lost item in the desert sands of Pinon Canyon maneuver site in southern Colorado, I received a frantic call on the radio of my Humvee vehicle. "Sir, we found it! Come to the BSA (Brigade Support Area)." My driver and I sped to the specified location, sensing relief that our long and seemingly futile search was over. Now we could get our 700+ soldiers back to work learning how to operate as a war fighting team.

Upon arrival at the BSA, I saw a large group of troops and leaders gathered around a bright blue "Porta Potty" (a field latrine). The company commander in charge escorted me to the center of this group. "Sir, our metal detector indicates that the lost item is inside the Porta Potty, down here." The point he indicated was well below the "water line" of this outhouse, and the entire group seemed paralyzed, transfixed on the dilemma they faced in retrieving the lost item from the mucky reservoir of the outdoor latrine.

I slowly rolled up the sleeves of my battle dress uniform.

"Sergeant Breedlove (my driver at the time), hand me the shovel."

As I shoveled "stuff" from the outhouse, I suddenly heard a promising metal clang. I then ceremoniously lifted out … a metal soft drink can! Although we continued the search for a number of days more, the battalion had learned much about their new battalion commander, a leader who was willing to "lead by example." Selfless Service over time from a platform of character and competence will often mean rolling your sleeves up and getting the job done, however distasteful.

Mobilize Resources

In addition to allowing subordinates to do their jobs in crisis, leaders should further empower them by mobilizing resources for their use. Often the tendency of inexperienced leaders is not to ask for external resources or support, coupled with failure to appreciate the true magnitude or implications of the crisis. The first question to such a leader who bears the burden of crisis should be "How are you doing?" It should be quickly followed by, "How can I help you? What do you need that you don't have?"

Often the more experienced senior leader can then mobilize resources from higher headquarters, partner organizations ("adjacent and supporting units" in military lingo), and technical entities that have specific technical skills to help with the crisis. In some of the actual crises we have referred to, this mobilization of external resources was a critical role for leaders and units in crisis. This dynamic holds true at every level of leadership authority ranging from squad leader to the most senior of military leaders, from shop foreman to the CEO in the boardroom. In the Fort Campbell drowning crisis, mobilizing diving crews to search for the soldier under the water was critical to the rescue and recovery operations. In the Fort Carson bus rollover, medical and public affairs support from the higher headquarters was pivotal in changing the public perception. In the Korean terrorist scenario, collaboration with the Defense Threat Reduction Agency (DTRA) in Washington, DC, and civil-military support from U.S. Forces Korea (USFK) were important resources that helped to abate the situation.

While the resources required will vary with each crisis, the principle is the same: In a true crisis, subordinate leaders need to ask for help, and quickly. Senior leaders need to mobilize external resources on behalf of their subordinates in crisis. In addition to asking, "How can I help you?" senior leaders must creatively and decisively use their direct and indirect influence to garner such help. Their success in this task will often depend upon the manner in which they have "set the conditions" with trusting working relationships with other leaders and other organizations before crisis occurs. Often this condition setting includes willingly helping others in their time of crisis.

This concludes our "best practice" discussion of leading others through a storm: positively affirm those in the crucible, let the experts do their job, seek historical parallels, shield subordinates, lead by example, and mobilize resources.

Now, let us consider one other example of leading in extremis, alluded to earlier in Chapter 5, when I assumed command of the Second Infantry Division in Korea.

Remember Nehemiah

"The Chief would like to speak with you. Please Stand By..."

Then Chief of Staff of the Army Dennis Reimer came on the line to inform me of a crisis in Korea:

"Bob, I would like for you to take command of 2nd Infantry Division on the Demilitarized Zone (DMZ) in Korea in nine days. We have to replace the current Division Commander for health reasons; in fact, he has been ineffective for a number of months... a real leadership crisis. By the way, the Division has just been hit by a powerful 100-year flood; five of your camps are devastated, your headquarters has been hit hard. We are concerned that the North Koreans might seek to take advantage of the situation; you must regain full readiness immediately."

So was my charter from the Army Chief of Staff to assume command of the Second Infantry Division in the Republic of South Korea in nine days. Kathleen (my dear wife who was listening nearby) and I dropped to our knees. "Lord, we can't do this." We knew how difficult such a task would be, and that normally the "pre-command" phase of preparation would last for a number of months. How could we possibly do this? But God reminded us, as He did the Apostle Paul, that "He is able and His grace is sufficient for all our needs."

"I am convinced that He is able to guard that what I have entrusted to him until that day." (2 Timothy 1:12)

"And He has said to me, 'My grace is sufficient for you, for power is perfected in weakness.' Most gladly, therefore, I will rather boast about my weaknesses, so that the power of Christ may dwell in me." (2 Corinthians 12:9)

Little did we know how true this would be.

In the few days of leader reflection before the change of command, God impressed upon me to "Remember Nehemiah." As I turned to the book of Nehemiah in the Old Testament, God unfolded the steps of a great biblical leader, which became my blueprint as I moved into Division command under the toughest of circumstances. Just as with Nehemiah returning from Babylon to rebuild the destroyed walls of Jerusalem, I saw that I would have to rebuild the physical and moral walls of the 'Second to None' Division. I applied the leadership principles directly:

- <u>Prayer is key</u>. A leader prays for his soldiers (Nehemiah 1:6). Prayer is powerful because it potentially changes the situation and it certainly changes the person who reaches out in prayer to the God of comfort and counsel.

- <u>Time spent in reconnaissance</u> is never wasted. Discretely assess the situation before you act (2:12).

- <u>Vision provides hope and direction</u>. "Let us arise and build!" (2:17) People must know your vision to make the project come to pass.

- <u>Teamwork is essential</u>. "We" built the wall; leaders build teams (2:18). Leadership is never a solo act.

- <u>Leaders will have opposition</u>. God of Heaven will grant success! (4:1-9:38) God is in the business of overcoming obstacles.

- <u>Security is paramount</u>. One hand on the weapon and one on the work means readiness! (4:9).

- <u>Leaders lead by example</u>. They did not eat the Governor's food allowance (5:13). If they had eaten it, they would have sacrificed the respect and allegiance of their followers. They would have sacrificed the moral high ground.

- Leaders model physical and moral courage. "Should a man like me flee? No!" (6:11)

- Commander and Chaplain are powerful partners. Note the working relationship between Nehemiah and Ezra (8:9). Seek and build strong alliances.

- Strong leaders share the victory. Leaders give the credit to God (worship and thankfulness) and others (honoring those to whom honor is due). (12:27)

Through this direct application of His Word, God provided me with wisdom, effectiveness, and confidence as a commander for over 19,000 soldiers on the DMZ in Korea. He allowed our team, assisted by many others, to restore combat readiness and to rebuild the physical infrastructure of the Division... over 612 engineering projects at a cost of $208 million dollars in less than a year. God allowed us to rebuild the moral infrastructure as well, restoring the bond of trust between the leader and those he leads, establishing high morale and a true sense of purpose. This was no doubt a "trial by fire," one which proved yet again that God's grace is truly sufficient, and His Bible is truly the world's greatest leadership manual.

Gaining Altitude

Crisis defines the character of the leader. During crisis, leaders must demonstrate sound character and technical competence to help their team "weather the storm." Growth as an "in extremis leader" is a lifelong endeavor. Unavoidably, learning about leading through crisis includes being in crisis.

There are many Biblical role models for leading in and through crisis. We have given examples of Jesus (calming the storm) and Nehemiah (rebuilding the wall). Additionally, we could profitably investigate Biblical leaders such as Joseph who, despite extremely unfair treatment, helped the nation of Egypt navigate a crisis of drought. Certainly a deeper examination of King Hezekiah would be equally profitable, dissecting his in extremis actions when faced with the daunting invasion by a coalition of foreign armies. There is a lifetime of leadership study in the scriptures alone, all providing invaluable insights and inspiration.

As well, you no doubt have observed inspiring contemporary role models who provided calm and confident leadership in a crisis, exactly what others needed. Who can forget President George Bush standing on top of the Twin Towers' smoldering embers to console workers and victims, and to inspire a nation? Similarly, we might think of Bernhard Baruch who mobilized our nation's industrial capacity to meet the demands of two world wars. Or perhaps General "Vinegar Joe" Stillwell who demonstrated great crisis leadership when fighting against insurmountable odds in Burma, led captives on the Bataan Death March, and provided inspired leadership while under Japanese captivity. These were also true resilient leaders.

May we emulate such role models, seeking to be resilient and resourceful leaders who can calm the storms of life for others and guide them to safe harbor.

> Crisis defines the character of the leader.

Now we move to the next phase of the Resilience Life Cycle© applied to resilient leadership: Chapter 7, "Leading After Crisis."

Resilient Leader Takeaways

RL 45 – Crisis Leaders honor the dead and lead the living.

RL 46 – Crisis Leaders positively affirm those in the crucible of crisis. They give life to confused, scared, and disconsolate followers.

RL 47 – Crisis Leaders know when to stay out of the way, letting experts do their job in time sensitive settings of urgency.

RL 48 – Crisis Leaders seek historical parallels. Someone has been here before! How did they handle it?

RL 49 – Crisis Leaders shield their subordinates from outside distractors, helping them focus on the crisis at hand.

RL 50 – Crisis Leaders lead by example, taking action when paralysis and fear have immobilized others.

RL 51 – Crisis Leaders mobilize external resources for the good of the cause, using their authority and influence to truly help their subordinates resolve the crisis.

RL 52 – Biblical and contemporary role models provide unlimited instruction and inspiration regarding crisis leadership. We should study them well.

Additional Study

1. Kolditz, Thomas A. *In Extremis Leadership*. San Francisco, CA: Jossey-Bass, 2007.

2. Ortberg, John. *If You Want to Walk on Water, You've Got to Get Out of The Boat*. Grand Rapids, MI: Zondervan, 2001.

7

I'd Rather Hide!
Leading After Crisis

As our youngest grandchild Kate neared her fifth birthday, our daughter, Allison, asked her what kind of a party she would like to have. Her fourth birthday had been a "pink party." Kate, a budding young ballerina who literally bounces around the stage, immediately proclaimed she wanted a "bounce party" for her fifth birthday. After ferreting out what that meant, our daughter then asked, "Who should we invite?" Again very decisively, Kate replied, "All girls, because boys don't bounce."

While I never quite figured out why "boys don't bounce," I did see that this humorous granddaughter vignette also told me that even young children intuitively value bounce. Bounce is an important characteristic for boys and girls, men and women, and especially military warriors and their families. In *Resilient Warriors* we dissected the Before-During-After of "bounce," or more succinctly, the Resilience Life Cycle©. We applied these concepts to each of us as individual resilient warriors. Specifically related to the "After" phase (after trauma, tribulation, body slams, wounds, broken relationships, dashed dreams, and great disappointments), we discussed how one "bounces back" without getting stuck in the negative emotions of guilt, false guilt, anger, bitterness, and lifelong remorse. *Resilient Warriors* readers will recall that we spent time discussing "Bouncing Back" (Guard Your Primary Relationships, Choose Forgiveness and Gratitude, and Grieve Well) and "Bouncing Ahead" (Sing a New Song, Revalidate Your Calling, and Comfort Others).

Now we will use parallel concepts to investigate how we as resilient <u>leaders</u> not only observe these principles individually, but also help those we lead and the organizations we direct to likewise rebound from challenges, reversals, and "cleverly disguised opportunities" towards a bright, hopeful, and productive future. How do we as leaders help our team look back at the challenges we endured? Specifically, how do we as leaders Rebuild the Team? Underwrite Mistakes? Mourn with Those Who Mourn? Then, helping the wounded team look forward, how do we as leaders: Be a Merchant of Hope? Revalidate the Team Azimuth? Empower Others?

As noted in *Resilient Warriors*, this "bounce back" phase is the most difficult part of the journey, for both leader and led. <u>Many times I truly wanted to hide</u> rather than face the tough tasks of grieving, rebuilding, and restoring hope. As a brief humorous intermission before we dive into serious discussion, you have probably heard a version of this account of a leader who wanted to hide:

(Wife to Husband) Honey, get up. It is time for Church!

(Husband) I don't want to get up!

(Wife to Husband) Honey, you really need to get up!

(Husband) Why? I just want to be by myself today.

(Wife to Husband) But Honey, you are the PASTOR!

Although they often prefer to hide, leaders are the only ones who can point the way to restoration and renewal. This is something resilient leaders can and must do.

Let's get started.

Rebuild the Team

Let's dive deeper into the example of Nehemiah that I outlined at the end of Chapter 6. Not only did Nehemiah model leadership during an initial crisis, he demonstrated the will and skill to help others "bounce back," successfully rebuilding the wall over a number of months under the most challenging of conditions. While there were many opportunities for the rebuilders of Jerusalem to become distracted from the work, Nehemiah's vision, wisdom, fortitude, and confidence in the cause led to a positive outcome. Here are a few examples of Nehemiah's resilient leadership:

- After conducting a horseback <u>reconnaissance</u> for three days and <u>maintaining discretion</u> regarding his assessment, he then went to his subordinate leaders and the people to <u>give them an accurate assessment</u> of the challenges they faced. He did not sugarcoat the reality of their situation. *"[17] Then I said to them, "You see <u>the bad situation we are in</u>, that <u>Jerusalem is desolate and its gates burned by fire</u>."* (Nehemiah 2:17a, underlines added)

- Although this was a situation where families and tribes could have turned against one another (similar to the tendency to turn on your own close relationships during tough personal trials, see Guard Your Primary Relationships in *Resilient Warriors*, pg 141), Nehemiah recognized it was critical to preserve a team approach, "all for one, and one for all." He emphasized "us" and "we" over "I" and "me." (As an aside, a leader who uses too many first person pronouns often unknowingly undercuts a spirit of unity and teamwork.)

  Because of his motivational approach, the "team" did not have to be ordered to do the work. Instead, <u>they</u> said, "Let us arise and build" and <u>they</u> "put their hands to the work." *"[17b]Come, <u>let us</u> rebuild the wall of Jerusalem so*

that we will no longer be a reproach.'" [18] *I told them how the hand of my God had been favorable to me and also about the king's words which he had spoken to me. Then they said, 'Let us arise and build.' So they put their hands to the good work."*
(Nehemiah 2:17b-18, underlines added)

- Nehemiah Chapter 3 records another important technique to preserve the team. He spelled out a very clear division-of-labor for each of the families, giving them well defined and achievable objectives related to their own place of residence, along with collective tasks to rebuild common areas. The manner in which a leader delegates and assigns tasks is critical to strengthening the team, particularly during the rebuilding phase.

- Nehemiah also overcame opposition as a resilient leader, giving his team courage and confidence. As well, he pointed his team and others to the "God of heaven."

[19] But when Sanballat the Horonite and Tobiah the Ammonite official and Geshem the Arab heard it, they mocked us and despised us and said, "What is this thing you are doing? Are you rebelling against the king?" [20] So I answered them and said to them, "The God of heaven will give us success; therefore we His servants will arise and build, but you have no portion, right or memorial in Jerusalem." (Nehemiah 2:19-20, underlines added)

As Nehemiah and the builders began to experience success, the opposition moved from mere words to threats of death and destruction, causing the builders to become demoralized:

> *"¹Now it came about that when Sanballat heard that we were rebuilding the wall, he became furious and very angry and mocked the Jews... ³ Now Tobiah the Ammonite was near him and he said, "Even what they are building—if a fox should jump on it, he would break their stone wall down!"*
>
> *⁴ᵃ Hear, O our God, <u>how we are despised!</u> Return their reproach on their own heads and give them up for plunder in a land of captivity... ⁵ Do not forgive their iniquity and let not their sin be blotted out before You, <u>for they have demoralized the builders</u>.*
>
> *⁶ <u>So we built the wall and the whole wall was joined together</u> to half its height, <u>for the people had a mind to work</u>.* [Parenthetical note: this phrase "the people had a mind to work" will be prominent consideration in the final book of the trilogy, *Resilient Nations*]
>
> *⁷ Now when Sanballat, Tobiah, the Arabs, the Ammonites and the Ashdodites heard that the repair of the walls of Jerusalem went on, and that the breaches began to be closed, they were very angry. ⁸ <u>All of them conspired together to come and fight against Jerusalem and to cause a disturbance in it</u>.* (Nehemiah 4:1, 3, 4a, and 5-8, underlines added)

I challenge you to dive deeper into the life and leadership of Nehemiah. He truly met the definition of "selfless service over time from a platform of character and competence." He also demonstrated well how to "Rebuild the Team" as he guided his organization in "bouncing back." We do well to follow his example.

A similar example worth emulating is required memorization for all plebes at West Point: Schofield's Definition of Discipline. While appropriate to many aspects of leadership, I cite it here because it parallels Nehemiah's approach to leadership so closely:

> *"The discipline which makes the soldiers of a free country reliable in battle is not to be gained by harsh or tyrannical treatment. On the contrary, such treatment is far more likely to destroy than to make an army.*
>
> *It is possible to impart instruction and to give commands in such a manner and such a tone of voice to inspire in the soldier no feeling but an intense desire to obey, while the opposite manner and tone of voice cannot fail to excite strong resentment and a desire to disobey. The one mode or the other of dealing with subordinates springs from a corresponding spirit in the breast of the commander. He who feels the respect which is due to others cannot fail to inspire in them regard for himself, while he who feels, and hence manifests, disrespect toward others, especially his inferiors,*

cannot fail to inspire hatred against himself."
(underlines added)
Major General John M. Schofield,
Address to the Corps of Cadets, August 11, 1879

One more topic worthy of mention as we conclude "Rebuild the Team" is personnel and key leader selection. After a seismic shock, the leader needs to ensure his team players are in the best role for them and for the team. This is always important, but in a rebuilding effort many of your leaders may have become physical or emotional casualties, you may have new insights into their ability to lead or perform, or the typical turbulence of the military and the business world may have sent many of your leaders to other roles. While large organizations typically spend considerable time on leader development, they often "underwhelm" the assessment of personnel prior to hiring. Said another way, "The best time to fire someone is <u>before</u> you hire them." While I have always thought this was important, my service alongside the Israeli Defense Forces (IDF) as the Commander for Operation Juniper Cobra (U.S. – Israeli Combined Task Force for Missile Defense) gave me the "picture worth a thousand words," although a humorous one as well.

One day the security officer at an Israeli airbase (location unspecified) asked me to take a ride with him. We'll call him Lieutenant Danny. I jumped in his Israeli "Sufa" (like an American Jeep) and we began to wind our way up a high plateau in the center of the airfield, overlooking the base in all directions. Arriving at the top, we stopped at the front door of an inconspicuous "shack," although it did have quite a few antennas on the top. As the IDF Lieutenant opened the door to the building, I was immediately greeted by three bouncy and beautiful girls in their late teens: "Hi, we're Danny's girls!" I noticed a couch on one wall with some bright pillows, as well as a poster of a rock star and some balloons hanging from the ceiling. Needless to say, I was beginning to wonder, thinking I had been transported back to my own daughter's teenage room.

"Girls, take the General to the back room," directed Danny. I warily stepped into the back room to find two more equally attractive young females. One of the girls then drew back a curtain on the far wall to reveal a bank of electronic boxes. I soon learned that these were listening devices, a hybrid of U.S. and Israeli technology that the Israelis had fine-tuned for the purpose of airbase security. One of the girls put on a set of headphones as Danny explained further.

"You see, General, these girls are all musical virtuosos. They have almost perfect pitch, timbre, tonal memory, and rhythm: four key measures of musical ability. They can detect the difference between human footsteps and an animal walking at (distance omitted) kilometers."

The IDF Lieutenant did not need to say more. I got it. The Israelis have such a small population that they must make the very best use of their human resources. They had correlated musical ability with the intelligence collection skills demanded by their security equipment, and had found the best IDF personnel for the job. This is what getting the right people in the right seats looks like.

Certainly U.S. military and business leaders can benefit from the same principle. The need to rebuild a team presents a "cleverly disguised opportunity" to achieve better alignment of our personnel resources with the necessary functions of our organizations. This is doubly important as we assess, select, empower, and grow leaders who will have impact on tens, thousands, or tens of thousands of others.

The need to rebuild a team presents a "cleverly disguised opportunity" to achieve better alignment of our personnel resources with the necessary functions of our organizations. This is doubly important as we assess, select, empower, and grow leaders who will have impact on tens, thousands, or tens of thousands of others.

Underwrite Mistakes

Recall my story from Chapter 1 regarding the needless drowning of my former RTO (radio telephone operator), the ensuing investigation, and my final exoneration from any punishment for the mishap. Reflecting further on the incident, I recognize that senior leadership could have easily ended my career, yet they extended "grace" to a young lieutenant who was still learning. I also recognized that as with Olympic competition, the "difficulty of the dive" is an important factor in assessing the shortfalls of others. In the rough and tumble world of business, parenting, teaching others, care giving, and most certainly military leadership with complex training scenarios and unpredictable battlefields, failure is a very possible outcome even for the very best of leaders. I am grateful that my senior leaders in those early years understood these dynamics.

Twenty-five years later, I found myself sitting behind my desk as the two-star Deputy Commander of V Corps, headquartered in Heidelberg, Germany. "Sir, Lieutenant Barton (name changed) is here for his Article 15 appeal," announced my aide. After taking responsibility for a really dumb action which had resulted in an Article 15 recommendation by the immediate command, the lieutenant basically laid himself on "the mercy of the court." As the final determiner of his fate, I knew that an Article 15 in his record would effectively end his short career. I also knew that the decision required great wisdom, achieving the right balance between upholding standards of performance and public perception of the officer corps, and allowing a young officer to make a non-career ending mistake.

In that moment, my mind turned back to the 15-6 Officer, Major Dan Campbell, who many years before had held Lieutenant Dees' fate in his hands. My moment of "grace received" in 1974 would become a moment of "grace given" in 2002:

> "Lieutenant Barton, I grant your Article 15 appeal.
> But more importantly, a few words of advice. You
> say you have learned from this. I firmly believe
> that you will fall the way you lean. If you have not

learned, if you do not purpose to change your inclination toward such behavior, then I know you will be standing in front of me again. If that happens, then the outcome will be sure and swift. Do you understand me? (Lieutenant Barton replies "Yes, Sir") That will be all."

Sometimes "investing" in a subordinate's serious mistake takes the form of grace (often defined as "unmerited favor"), forgiving and underwriting their mistakes in order for them to learn. Assuming the young leader truly wants to learn and improve, such investments by a more senior leader can pay big dividends. As this is being written, Lieutenant Barton is now Lieutenant <u>Colonel</u> Barton, a skilled leader responsible for the lives of many soldiers and families. His "grace received" has no doubt motivated him to likewise invest in others.

"Mourn with Those Who Mourn"

While it is important for an outfit to quickly move past tragedy and trauma, it is also naive for a leader to not understand that grieving and healing take time. In His Sermon on the Mount, Jesus said, *"Blessed are those who mourn, for they shall be comforted."* (Matthew 5:4) Paul highlights the leader and caregiver side of this when he further exhorts, *"Rejoice with those who rejoice; mourn with those who mourn."* (Romans 12:15) In the aftermath of crisis and trauma, the wise leader knows how and when to mourn with his team. Certainly when the dense fog of pain and suffering lies heavy upon troops and their families, leaders must manifest the right spirit of "mourning with those who mourn." This is a time for leaders to be present, for leaders to comfort, for leaders to listen and love.

The greater challenge comes days, weeks, and months after trauma strikes an organization. This is when an insensitive remark or action by a leader can often trigger a deeply emotional response (seen or unseen) in the heart of the grief bearer. As well as on the personal level, an organization has a memory which never forgets the deep pain suffered by its members. While we can certainly understand the lifelong grief of a prominent tragedy such as Pearl Harbor, it is often easier to forget that our own organization has (or certainly will have) deeply emotional markers in its own history. Leaders who guide organizations out of trial and tribulation do well to remember this.

As well as on the personal level, an organization has a memory which never forgets the deep pain suffered by its members.

A very palpable example of the above is memorialization of the Gander, Newfoundland civilian air transport crash which decimated a battalion task force (primarily 3-502 Infantry) of 101st Airborne troops returning from Sinai Peacekeeping duty on December 12, 1985, killing all 248 members of the task force (and eight crew members) who were headed home to cheering families at Fort Campbell, Kentucky. Wise senior leaders in the

101st Airborne, at higher levels of command, and in the local communities certainly wrapped their arms around troops, families, and one another during those difficult days following the crash. They also provided fitting memorials for decades to follow. Today, twenty-seven years later, as you drive along Screaming Eagle Boulevard at Fort Campbell, you will see a stately formation of 256 tall Canadian Maple trees, one for each fallen warrior. On December 12 every year, there is a sober wreath laying ceremony around the Gander monument at this memorial site. Today, as you drive from Fort Campbell into Hopkinsville, Kentucky you will see the prominent Stars and Stripes flag which dominates the day and night horizons, maintaining vigilance over the Hopkinsville Gander Memorial Park. As well, there is a fitting memorial overlooking Gander Lake vicinity, the site of the crash in Newfoundland, Canada.

These far-sighted efforts to memorialize the fallen from the Gander Crash and to empathize with their survivors are fitting and proper examples of how to "mourn with those who mourn." Life certainly goes on at Fort Campbell, but the memorial symbols on and off post are a constant reminder of the nobility and the sacrifice of those who gave all. These symbols instill a degree of humanity and compassion into the tough profession of soldiering, certainly befitting Tom Kolditz' conclusion cited in Chapter 6: "Honor the Dead, Lead the Living."

While these examples above are lifted directly from military life, the principle is common to all professions and life experiences. Consider business leaders who lost employees and entire organizations in the Twin Towers on September 11, or church leaders who experienced walk-in shootings or the fall of a prominent pastor, or community leaders dealing with the aftermath of a Hurricane Katrina or a Superstorm Sandy, or the family unit who suffers the breakdown of a loved relationship, or many other examples in your own life experience. We all have tribulation, and we must all rebuild in various ways. This includes "mourning with those who mourn."

Be a Merchant of Hope

A "merchant of hope" is one who conveys a sense that things will get better, a sense that current trials will result in future benefit for self and others, a sense that we ultimately will not be disappointed. A merchant of hope does not deny present suffering for himself and others, yet he conveys optimism, helping others hold on for a better tomorrow.

It is important that leaders serve as merchants of hope, particularly following traumatic events in an organization. President George Bush and New York City Mayor Rudy Giuliani were merchants of hope in the early days after 911. Colin Powell in *It Worked for Me* (page 3) provides his "Rules" which include Rule #13 "Perpetual Optimism is a Force Multiplier." Similarly, we remember President Ronald Reagan's reminder that "The Best is Yet to Come." Or you may have heard that optimism is the ability to see a "glass half full" (instead of half empty). Optimism is a key quality for leaders that helps them be merchants of hope.

On Sunday, December 7, 1941 (the evening of Pearl Harbor Day), Admiral Chester Nimitz was attending a concert in Washington, D.C.   Receiving a phone from President Roosevelt, he was informed that he would now be the Commander of the Pacific Fleet. After preparations for this responsibility, Admiral Nimitz arrived at Pearl Harbor on Christmas Eve, 1941. He found a spirit of despair, dejection, and defeat—you would have thought the Japanese had already won the war. On Christmas Day, he was given a boat tour of the sunken battleships and Navy vessels which had become tombs for over 3800 sailors caught in the surprise attack. The young helmsman of the boat asked him, "Well, Admiral, what do you think after seeing all this destruction?" Admiral Nimitz's optimistic reply was shocking to those gathered: "The Japanese made three of the biggest mistakes an attack force could ever make... God was really taking care of America." He continued to explain that 1) the Japanese attacked on Sunday morning when most crewmen were on shore on leave (otherwise we might have lost 38,000 sailors), 2) the Japanese never attacked the dry docks we will use to repair our ships (allowing them to be repaired quickly), and 3) the Japanese did not attack our fuel supply (one attack plane could have strafed the fuel tanks and destroyed the entire fuel supply).

Admiral Nimitz was able to see the silver lining in a dire situation where others could only see despair and defeat. He was a true merchant of hope. President Roosevelt had chosen the right resilient leader for the job.

Ultimately, optimism is an outer display of the inner quality of hope. If one is hopeful, they can more readily look positively, optimistically, toward the future. While trial and tribulation often bring about human despair and anguish, the Biblical thread of God's redemptive purposes for us and others allows one to maintain hope for the future. Romans Chapter 5 highlights the redemptive purposes of tribulation which lead to perseverance, character, hope and an overall mindset of optimism:

> "[2b]... we exult in hope of the glory of God. [3] And not only this, but we also exult in our *tribulations, knowing that <u>tribulation brings about perseverance</u>;* [4] *and perseverance, <u>proven character</u>; and proven character, <u>hope</u>;* [5] *and <u>hope does not disappoint</u>, because the love of God has been poured out within our hearts through the Holy Spirit who was given to us."*
> (Romans 5:2b-5, underlines added)

Given the relevance of hope and optimism to resilient leaders, here are a few more Biblical verses which further highlight the power of hope:

- An Antidote to Despair
  "Why are you in despair, O my soul? And why have you become disturbed within me? <u>Hope in God</u>, for I shall yet praise Him, The help of my countenance and my God." (Psalm 42:15, underline added)

- Hope through Prayer
  "For I hope in you, O LORD; <u>you will answer</u>, O Lord my God." (Psalm 38:15)

- A Source of Confidence
  "For You are my hope; O Lord GOD, You are <u>my confidence</u> from my youth?"
  (Psalm 71:5, underline added)

- Linked to Perseverance and Encouragement
  "For whatever was written in earlier times was written for our instruction, so that <u>through perseverance and the encouragement of the Scriptures</u> we might have hope.
  (Romans 15:4, underline added)

- Source of Boldness
  "Therefore, having such hope, we use <u>great boldness</u> in our speech..."
  (I Corinthians 3:12, underline added)

- An Anchor for the Soul
  "... we who would have taken refuge would have <u>strong encouragement</u> to take hold of the hope set before us. This hope we have as <u>an anchor of the soul</u>, a hope both <u>sure and steadfast</u> ..."
  (Hebrews 6:18b-19a, underlines added)

> Ultimately, optimism is an outer display
> of the inner quality of hope.

Which of us as leaders do not need full measure of these qualities that result from hope? Which of us would not want the same qualities in those we lead?

This hope that we need as leaders is not the result of some "feel good" mindset that is self-generated. Those surface emotions are often short lived in the face of incoming bullets, or other challenges in life. Although there are many sources of hope, the deep foundational source is God. For followers of Christ, this comes through the person of Jesus.

The leader who is confident in the ultimate source of his hope and who is able to convey this optimism-generating hope to others truly is a "force multiplier," a merchant of hope.

Revalidate Your Team's Azimuth and Processes

An organizational setback is another "cleverly disguised opportunity" to start anew, to restore clarity and freshness to stale vision, mission, and goal statements. Often the searing reality of trauma makes people more open to new ideas, new ways to do business, new ways to move forward, and a new commitment to just say "No" to non-essential commitments that may have grown over time, sapping energy and focus from your organization. We made this point on the personal level in Chapter 8 of *Resilient Warriors* as we discussed "Revalidate Your Call."

As a young infantry officer in the days before GPS (Global Positioning System) greatly simplified land navigation, I spent a lot of time with a map and compass. From the map you would determine the "azimuth" (say 270 degrees, which is due west) and distance to the desired destination from their present location.

As well you would <u>do a thorough "map reconnaissance,"</u> the ounce of prevention worth a pound of cure. For example: uphill for 300 meters, then downhill for 200 meters with the river just on our left, then level ground for 400 meters to an intersection of two dirt roads... you get the picture! Then you would <u>set this azimuth</u> on your magnetic pocket compass, along with keeping track of distance traveled via your "pace count" (the number of your steps to cover a known distance, usually measured in 100 meter intervals). When navigating under realistic conditions, such as at night over rough terrain and perhaps enemy threat, the wise leader will <u>make frequent navigation checks</u>, as well as using other indicators such as <u>"terrain association"</u> (does the terrain you see look like what you would expect from your map reconnaissance?). As part of my early training with land navigation using a compass, I quickly learned that a slight variation in azimuth would cause a serious error over distance. For instance, <u>being "off azimuth" just one degree</u> would result in being off course laterally by roughly 18 meters after traveling only 1,000 meters. <u>And the error gets greater with further distance</u>. Certainly being "off azimuth" is not a good thing for a young infantry officer with a platoon of thirty soldiers in tow.

Being "off azimuth" is detrimental to any organization. The basics of land navigation we have discussed above apply equally well to "revalidating your team's azimuth and processes," particularly useful after the organization has experienced crisis, downturn, or stagnation. A couple of brief comments in this regard:

The "map" is critical, as is a detailed "map reconnaissance." Wise leaders study and assess the "terrain" that they must navigate, including market conditions, future projections, and potential obstacles and opportunities along the way. Some would call this a "SWOT Analysis" (Strengths, Weaknesses, Opportunities, and Threats). As we discussed in Chapter 4 (Wisdom), wise leaders need to emulate the men of Issachar who "understood the times, and knew the direction (azimuth) Israel should go." (I Chronicles 12:32) This is a critical first step in "Revalidating Azimuth" for an organization which is seeking to "bounce back."

"Setting the azimuth" is an important next step, implying the alignment of organizational processes in support of the desired direction, distance, and pace which the leader (and his supporting staff) determines to be best for the organization. This often includes re-firing old processes, as well as establishing new ones. It also involves putting metrics in place that allow leadership to monitor progress. In Second Infantry Division, for instance, we had to revamp our "risk management" process in order to reduce the unacceptably high incidence of training accidents.

Frequent navigation checks and terrain association equate in a broader sense to periodic "pulse checks" to ensure that you are on plan. Leaders should integrate periodic reviews into the life of their organization, aimed at answering key questions:

- Are we on plan?
- Have market conditions changed?
- Do we need to make a mid-course correction to our current azimuth?

An organizational "battle rhythm" (now a familiar term which is used across many domains, originally coined in a 1987 *Military Review* article entitled "Battle Rhythm" by then Major Bob Dees) helps leaders proactively "look over the horizon" in a planning sense to better anticipate the way ahead and ensure the organizational azimuth is still "on target." Here is a short extract from my thoughts in 1987 which laid out the premise for battle rhythm:

> "Battle rhythm is based upon the principle that it takes far less time and energy to redirect an object which is already moving than to start a stationary object. Examples abound. The flywheel of a car overcomes the inherent inertia of the motor and allows for rapid acceleration. The spinning of a gyroscope allows for the fluidity of motion in a spaceship. The rhythmic beat of a drum and well-understood calls of cadence make possible the coordinated mass action of a marching army. In each case, a repetitive process, a rhythm, is key to the success of the machine or the organization. This concept of rhythm directly applies to combat organizations (and all other organizations)—hence, battle rhythm."
> (page 59, parenthetical comments added)

> "Sir Isaac Newton's first law of motion maintains that an object at rest tends to stay at rest, and an object in motion tends to stay in motion. This is also true of military organizations

(as well as all other types of organizations). Each unit must develop a battle rhythm which keeps it "in motion"—able to quickly seize upon opportunities to gain or maintain the initiative."
(page 64, parenthetical comments added)

"Initiative has two components—physical and intellectual. Battle rhythm is particularly linked to the intellectual initiative as it <u>forces planning and decisions under uncertainty using predictive intelligence</u> (military intelligence, or equally applicable to business intelligence). These <u>timely decisions</u> allow for proactive combat (or business operations) rather than reactive combat. The result is the aggressive execution of flexible plans and a confused enemy whose next step has been anticipated and disrupted. The initiative has been seized!"
(page 64, parenthetical comments and underlines added)

An intentional organizational battle rhythm is an important technique to help leaders periodically "revalidate their azimuth" and to proactively identify and shape emerging conditions even before the storm clouds form. While the frequency and exact approach may vary, I have found it essential for an organization's battle rhythm to include regularly scheduled "strategic moments" which force the organization to revalidate azimuth. In an operational military setting, this could take the form of a daily "deep battle" update. In a peacetime or business setting, this might be a quarterly "strategic offsite" lasting one or more days. For additional information regarding battle rhythm, simply conduct an Internet search to see the wide variety of potential applications.

To summarize this section, crisis in any form becomes a "teachable moment" for an organization. Organizational "bounce back" includes "Revalidating the Azimuth" to ensure that energy applied to recovery is well focused and pointed in the right direction. This includes developing a keen appreciation of current and anticipated (future) market conditions ("understanding the times") as well as developing a proactive battle rhythm which helps to foresee and shape the future.

Empower Others

Earlier in our discussion of "condition setting" (Chapter 5), I mentioned the "voice in the dark" acid test which I gave to my leaders in Korea. As well, we covered a second acid test: "Do you know your troops?" A third acid test I challenged them with was:

"Do your troops know that you need them?"

This question highlights the importance of the leader em-powering and valuing each team member.

Setting the stage, we were playing artillery cat and mouse games with the North Koreans. In 1998, on the other side of the world in Kuwait and Iraq, there had been a dust-up with Saddam

Hussein requiring greater intelligence assets. The National Command Authority (NCA) had transferred significant intelligence capabilities (satellites, high altitude reconnaissance planes, and analytic priority) to Iraq, bleeding intelligence capability off of the Korean peninsula. At that point in time the North Koreans, not being unaware of this, started to reposition many of their deeply buried artillery locations that we had pinpointed over decades. All of a sudden, all bets were off. We had far less certainty about where their weapons were located, meaning that our deterrent capability and our ability to accurately respond to North Korean fires was significantly degraded. This was a serious security threat for the nation of South Korea and for the U.S. forces stationed there.

I called the commander of our Second Infantry Division (2ID) Division Artillery, Colonel Jim Church, and said, "Jim, we need to figure this out... and fast! Take a few days and I'll fly over to Camp Stanley for a laydown (military vernacular for an analysis of mission, enemy, terrain, troops available, and time) and some recommendations." Hindered by the significant personnel turbulence characteristic of a theater such as Korea with one year tours, this situation could not have come at a worse time for Jim Church—the artillery Major in charge of intelligence preparation of the battlefield had rotated out the past week, as well as a number of other key players on that team. When I arrived at Division Artillery Headquarters a few days later, I found a young and inexperienced female sergeant (SGT) as the primary briefer. As I learned later, she was planning to leave the Army after several demotivating assignments.

After a very extensive enemy artillery laydown and good recommendations regarding how we should address the intelligence gaps that needed to be addressed, I quickly recognized that this was a profound moment, not just from a war fighting angle but also from a leadership perspective. The young SGT who briefed me (necessitated by the absence of other more experienced staff members) gave the effort her best, and it was very good. It was in fact better than the departed Major had ever done, or anyone else for that matter. For the first time in her military career, she felt like she had been part of the team, she had been entrusted with significant responsibility, she had been needed. What a change in attitude and motivation! What a lift to know that she could be an asset to the team! What a paradigm shift for the follower who suddenly discovered that she had an important role to play!

Oh, by the way, this young SGT reenlisted in the Army soon thereafter, serving with renewed motivation, recognizing that she was valuable to her leadership. When Colonel Jim Church entrusted this young soldier with such a challenging task and empowered her with the resources to get it done, he gave her new life. He made her a part of the team, which means everything.

No doubt you have seen this same dynamic in your own world of leadership. I know I have, time and again. I've seen soldiers go from zero to sixty, from demoralized to literally giving their lives for you, just because they know they are needed. They know they count for something.

So where does this principle of empowering the members of your team come from? Where did this acid test, *"Do your troops know that you need them?"* come from? For me, it came from one of the great fishing stories in the Bible in John Chapter 21. Let me set the stage.

Having retreated to the Sea of Galilee somewhat discouraged and uncertain about the future (sort of like the young intelligence SGT), the disciples reverted back to the familiar wind, waves, smells, and sounds. "Simon Peter said to them, 'I am going fishing.' They said to him, 'We will also come with you.' They went out and got into the boat; and that night they caught nothing." (John 21:3, underline added) Here we have experienced fishermen who knew the wind and the waves; they had done this a thousand times, always hauling in fish. Yet, they caught nothing. Personally demoralizing? Yes!

To summarize the next six verses (John 21:4-9), Jesus appeared on the beach as dawn was breaking, although not yet recognized by the discouraged fishermen disciples. Still un-recognized, He simply told them to cast their net on the right side of the boat. You can hear Peter thinking, "Who is this stranger who is telling us professional fishermen how to do their job?" Yet the disciples complied and their net was filled with a great draft of fish which they could not haul into the boat. Peter recognized Jesus on the shore, threw himself into the sea, and headed to Jesus. The other disciples remained in the boat, rowing and dragging the overflowing net of fish to shore. When they got on land, the disciples saw a charcoal fire already laid and fish placed on it, and bread.

Then, the profound words and acts of a wise leader...

"Bring some of the fish which you have now caught."
(John 21:10, underline added)

In essence, Jesus chose to use their fish, "...which you have now caught." Isn't that interesting? He is going to take his "divine fish" off the fire, so to speak, and He is going to use their imperfect fish, the fish that they have caught. Basically He is saying, bring your hopes, your gifts, your dreams, your aspirations—I choose to use you, I choose to need you, I empower you. That is incredibly powerful leadership dynamic, when the leader is sufficiently vulnerable, the leader tells others that he needs their efforts, he reinforces them as team members, and he puts them in the fight.

The applications are numerous for all of us—as marriage partners, as parents, as bosses, as followers, as coaches across every endeavor of life.

Do your "troops" know that you need them? Great leaders empower others, particularly when they are helping their organization bounce back, when they are breathing new life into followers and teams who have experienced challenging times.

Gaining Altitude

The only aspect of the Resilience Life Cycle© which we have not examined directly from a resilient leader perspective is the feedback loop, "Learn and Adapt." We have, however, discussed many factors surrounding personal and organizational growth which directly apply to this <u>intentional capture of life and organizational lessons which leads to adaptation</u>. The reality is that "Learn and Adapt" is a continuous process occurring across all parts of the Resilience Life Cycle©, ideally happening all the time in individual lives and in organizations.

I talked in earlier chapters about the U.S. Army's transformation into a learning organization. Although I highlighted the value of laser technology in this transformation, the real motivating force was a cultural change that embraced healthy introspection as an implicit core value. For the transforming Army, the National Training Center (NTC) was the venue in which tough, realistic training intersected with rigorous and healthy assessment of outcomes and corrective actions. The AAR ("After Action Review") became an institutionalized practice and an organizational mindset at every level and in every corner of the Army, and the same methodology spread to the other military Services, government agencies, and across to the business sector. The focus of any AAR is an objective assessment of the basic questions:

What was expected to happen?

What actually occurred?

What went well, and why?

What can be improved, and how?

I found that the most powerful AARs were the ones where the leader volunteered his own shortcomings, modeling candor and a teachable spirit for others. This usually led to equal introspection by others and a collaborative knowledge transfer which strengthened future performance and strengthened the team.

Let us not overlook the broad applicability of such best practices in the world of business, education, public and private sector service, parenting, and any other domain where learning and adapting is crucial. I am hard pressed to name any area of endeavor that does not benefit from such introspection and adaptation. Whether the AAR is in a mobile van at the National Training Center, or on the shop floor of a factory, or in the home over spilt milk; this ethic of <u>learning</u> from life experiences and <u>adapting</u> to meet future demands lies at the heart of resilient life and leadership.

We started this chapter by recognizing that crisis, reversals, opposition often make leaders want to hide. But resilient leaders don't have that option. They make a difference, particularly when others need inspiration, when others need to know what to do next, when others need courage, when the team needs to bounce back.

Guiding a team or large organization through the bounce back from daunting challenges is difficult, but certainly achievable. Techniques such as those discussed here can help resilient leaders make this journey: Rebuild The Team, Underwrite Mistakes, Mourn With Those Who Mourn, Be A Merchant Of Hope, Revalidate Your Team's Azimuth And Processes, and Empower

Others. Role models are also instructive: Nehemiah, General Schofield, Admiral Nimitz, and, of course, Jesus.

We also introduced one other acid test of leadership in this chapter, namely:

Do your troops know that you need them?

Regardless of how "troops" is defined for each of us, may we as resilient leaders empower others with the knowledge that they are unique, valuable, and important to the team. Then we will have the privilege of observing the commitment, sacrifice, and exceptional service of those who know that they matter.

Now we move from "Bouncing Back" to "Careful Your Well of Courage!" in Chapter 8, focusing on how leaders stay in the fight over time, consistent with our definition of resilient leadership as "selfless service <u>over time</u> from a platform of character and competence." How do leaders care for themselves so that they might continue to care for others?

Resilient Leader Takeaways

RL 53 – <u>Many times leaders want to hide</u> during the most challenging "bounce back" phase, rather than facing the tough tasks of grieving, rebuilding, regaining momentum, and renewing hope. Resilient leaders are the ones who can and must guide their team through this season of restoration and growth.

RL 54 – In <u>rebuilding the team</u> after a seismic shock has rocked the organization, the resilient leader needs to seize the opportunity to revalidate that his players are in the optimal role for them and for the team, ensuring best alignment of personnel resources with the necessary functions of the organization.

RL 55 – In the rough and tumble world of business, parenting, teaching others, care giving, and most certainly military leadership with complex training scenarios and unpredictable battlefields, failure is a very possible outcome even for the very best of leaders. Resilient leaders must <u>underwrite mistakes</u> as a key means to growing future leaders.

RL 56 – While it is important for an outfit to quickly move past tragedy and trauma, it is also naive for a leader to not understand that grieving and healing take time. When the dense fog of pain and suffering lies heavy upon troops and their families, resilient leaders must <u>mourn with those who mourn</u>.

RL 57 – A resilient leader who is a <u>merchant of hope</u> does not deny present suffering for himself and others, yet he conveys optimism, helping others hold on for a better tomorrow.

RL 58 – Organizational bounce back includes <u>revalidating the azimuth</u> to ensure that energy applied to recovery is well focused and pointed in the right direction. This includes developing a <u>keen appreciation of current and future</u>

market conditions as well as developing a proactive battle rhythm which helps to foresee and shape the future.

RL 59 – Do your troops know that you need them? is a condition setter which emphasizes team. Resilient leaders empower others, particularly when they are helping their organization bounce back, when they are breathing new life into followers and teams who have experienced challenging times.

RL 60 – The ethic of learning from life experiences and adapting to meet future demands lies at the heart of resilient life and leadership.

Additional Study

1. Tillman, Spencer. *Scoring in the Red Zone: How to Lead Successfully When the Pressure Is On.* Nashville, TN: Thomas Nelson, 2005. [Note: an in-depth discussion of Nehemiah's leadership]

2. Irwin, Tim. *Run with the Bulls without Getting Trampled.* Nashville, TN: Thomas Nelson, 2006.

3. Manion, Jeff. *The Land Between.* Grand Rapids, MI: Zondervan, 2010.

4. Powell, Colin, and Klotz, Tony. *It Worked For Me in Life and Leadership.* New York, NY: Harper Collins, 2012.

8

"Careful Your Well of Courage!"
Leader Self-Care

"Careful you don't dip too deeply
Into your Well of Courage"
General Dick Cavazos, U.S. Army, Retired

General Dick Cavazos, quoted above, was a very experienced combat commander and a wise leader. When referring to Well of Courage, he was talking about observing men under fire who suddenly found their physical, emotional, spiritual reservoir empty when faced with yet another life-threatening situation for themselves or others. His metaphor is apt. The reality is that we all have a reservoir, a well of courage, which is limited in capacity and must be refilled to avoid depletion.

As leaders who seek excellence over time and resilience when the chips are down, we are confronted with some fundamental questions: What depletes my well of courage? How do I measure it? What refills it? How often must I refuel? How long does it take? Although we are all different, this chapter will address some common denominators toward ensuring that we "serve selflessly OVER TIME from a platform of character and competence."

The Bible also addresses this leader challenge of self-care. Hebrews 12:1 reminds us that we have the encouragement of many role models who have paved the way for us (a "great cloud of witnesses") and that we all have obstacles and sin which stand in our way. It exhorts us as leaders to run this challenging race (unique to each one of us) with endurance:

> "[1]Therefore, since we have so <u>great a cloud of witnesses</u> surrounding us, let us also <u>lay aside every encumbrance and the sin which so easily entangles us</u>, and let us <u>run with endurance</u> the race that is set before us," (underlines added)

Hebrews 12:2-3a reminds us of the ultimate example and inspiration we have in Jesus:

> "[2] <u>fixing our eyes on Jesus</u>, the author and perfecter of faith, who for the joy set before Him endured the cross, despising the shame, and has sat down at the right hand of the throne of God. [3a] For

consider Him who has <u>endured such hostility</u> by sinners against Himself," (underlines added)

Concluding with the desired end state, that our "well of courage" does not run dry, Hebrew 12:3b states this succinctly:

"[3b]so that you will <u>not grow weary</u> (physical, mental, emotional exhaustion) <u>and lose heart</u> (become discouraged or burned out)." (underlines and parenthetical comments added)

"How do we not grow weary and lose heart as leaders?" is one of the most relevant questions of our time and critical to the subject of resilient leadership. Leader "burnout" abounds. "Compassion Fatigue" is prevalent among caregivers. "Dropout" rates are unacceptably high among chaplains, pastors, mission- aries, and other serving professions. "Self-Care" is a lost art in our Western society in particular.

The primary contributing factor to this trend is undoubtedly the increased tempo of our modern information age where the twenty-four hour news cycle constantly invades our collective consciousness while our personal digital devices continuously disrupt our individual solitude. The result is an "ADD society" (referring to "attention deficit disorder") which has mistaken multi-tasking with productivity. We do this at our own peril, subjecting ourselves to unnecessary stress and risking personal relationships through our inattentiveness to others. As well, leader fatigue and disillusionment (causing anger, blaming, sleeplessness, loss of passion, et al) threaten the emotional stability and the relational health (family, friends, and fellow workers) of the bedraggled leader.

Resilient leaders know how to counteract these continual stressors in order to stay in the game. In this chapter we will explore some principles and practices of leader self-care which will help us be more resilient leaders.

As a start, we should better characterize stress and its companion burnout. Dr. Archibald Hart, Senior Professor of Psychology and Dean Emeritus, Department of Clinical Psychology at Fuller University, provides a better understanding of burnout and stress, and a contrast between the two in his couplets below:

- *"Burnout* is a defense mechanism characterized by *disengagement*.
- *Stress* is characterized by *over-engagement*.

- In *Burnout*, the emotions become *blunted*.
- In *Stress*, the emotions become *over-active*.

- In *Burnout*, the *emotional* damage is primary.
- In *Stress*, the *physical* damage is primary.

- The exhaustion of *Burnout* affects *motivation and drive*.
- The exhaustion of *Stress* affects *physical energy*.

- *Burnout* produces *demoralization*.
- *Stress* produces *disintegration*.

- *Burnout* can best be understood as a loss of *ideals and hope*.
- *Stress* can best be understood as a loss of *fuel and energy*.

- *Burnout* produces a sense of *helplessness* and *hope-lessness*.
- *Stress* produces a sense of *urgency* and *hyperactivity*.

- *Burnout* produces *paranoia*, *depersonalization*, and *detachment*.
- *Stress* produces *panic*, *phobia*, and *anxiety*.

- *Burnout* may *never kill you*, but your long life may not seem worth living.
- *Stress* may *kill you prematurely*, and you won't have enough time to finish what you started."

I suspect after reading these characterizations that you and I recognize the need to avoid burnout at all costs and reduce negative stressors which in the aggregate can result in burnout (an empty well of courage). Hence, an important caution to resilient leaders is "Careful Your Well of Courage!" The leader competency to offset this danger is "leader self-care" which avoids the pitfalls of both burnout and excessive stress.

A fitting analogy to illustrate leader self-care occurs every time we take a plane trip. You have heard the flight attendant say many times before takeoff: "In the case of loss of cabin pressure, an oxygen mask will drop from above your seat. Put on the mask (as she or he demonstrates). In the case you are traveling with children or small infants, <u>put on your mask first, then assist others</u>." In this context, we clearly understand that to help others we must first help ourselves. Yet frequently as leaders, we help ourselves last, if ever.

I saw the importance of self-care first hand when I was a new battalion commander at Fort Carson. After an extended field operation (some of which I have described earlier), I had just returned to my office in the battalion headquarters as the battalion was going through the first stages of recovery (accounting for all sensitive items, initial cleaning of weapons and other equipment, completion of any incident reports, etc.) before being released to the waiting arms of family and friends. The battalion intelligence officer (S2) came into my office to gather some maps and follow up on some earlier questions. While talking to him, my sleep-deprived words literally became gibberish. The S2 kindly suggested "Sir, maybe you should lie down for a few minutes." I crashed on my office couch under a poncho liner and woke up two hours later as a different person. I had flown myself into the ground and literally become dys-functional as a leader. Gratefully, this early experience helped me to better appreciate the value of self-care for me and those I lead.

Another personal reminder regarding self-care occurred during a recent trip to the West Coast when I received an impromptu request to speak at a Veterans' Home that was en route to one of our other meetings. My hosts were sure I would agree to the added event, having seen my passion to encourage veterans many times before. Yet, I surprised them, and myself, when I simply said, "I don't think we are going to do that today."

I had recognized that my own "well of courage" was very low and that one more, simple event would likely be the "straw that broke the camel's back." I remember this instance vividly because one of my Achilles' heels as a leader has been not saying "No" often enough. Perhaps you are afflicted with the same issue.

How then do we take care of ourselves as leaders, keeping ourselves in the fight and modeling an important leader competency for others? WITH THE BASIC ASSUMPTION THAT MAINTAINING DAILY DISCIPLINES to achieve Comprehensive Personal Fitness™ (physical, mental, spiritual, emotional, relational) is the ESSENTIAL FIRST STEP to leader self-care, let me provide a few additional "best practices" which have proved beneficial to me and others.

... to help others we must first help ourselves.

Comprehensive Self-Care™

In *Resilient Warriors* we introduced the concept of Comprehensive Personal Fitness™ (CPF) based upon the Great Commandment in Mark 12. In discussing Selflessness in Chapter 2 of this book, we used the Luke version which immediately precedes the story of the Good Samaritan:

> [25] And a lawyer stood up and put Him to the test, saying, "Teacher, what shall I do to inherit eternal life?" [26] And He said to him, "What is written in the Law? How does it read to you?" [27] And he answered, "YOU SHALL LOVE THE LORD YOUR GOD WITH ALL YOUR HEART (emotional), AND WITH ALL YOUR SOUL(spiritual), AND WITH ALL YOUR STRENGTH (physical), AND WITH ALL YOUR MIND (mental); AND YOUR NEIGHBOR AS YOURSELF (relational)." [28] And He said to him, "You have answered correctly; DO THIS AND YOU WILL LIVE."
> (Luke 10:25-28, parenthetical comments added)

This Great Commandment highlights the Physical, Mental, Spiritual, Emotional, and Relational domains in developing resilience, which we also used for the *Resilient Warriors* segment on "Revalidate Your Calling" (Chapter 8). As we now look at the subject of leader self-care, this same Comprehensive Personal Fitness™ paradigm will serve us well. We will call this Comprehensive Self-Care™.

Dr. Michael Lyles, a very competent psychiatrist in Atlanta, GA, a Board Member of the American Association of Christian Counselors (AACC), and a nationally recognized expert on the subject of self-care discussed the following health guidelines with fellow counselors at a recent AACC Conference (aligned in Comprehensive Self-Care™ categories):

- **Physical**: sleep, diet, exercise, hygiene (including regular flossing because of the direct correlation with heart disease), supplements, and "know your numbers" (referring to blood pressure, cholesterol, et al)
- **Mental:** continue academic pursuits, intellectual growth
- **Spiritual:** avoid "spiritual narcissism" (needing to be needed, rather than truly loving God with pure motives)
- **Emotional:** seek balance by leaving work at work, pursuing hobbies, and taking time to "smell the roses"
- **Relational:** importance of friends, including accountable relationships with someone who doesn't call you Doctor or Reverend or General

While Dr. Lyles (and probably each of us) could add volumes to each individual category above, these main points of emphasis address what he recognizes to be key points of leader self-care vulnerability. For me (and perhaps true for most military professionals), the last two categories (Emotional and Relational, significantly interwoven) are the toughest self-care disciplines to observe. I will refer to these multiple times in our next section on "disciplines of replenishment."

Disciplines of Replenishment

While major periods of downtime such as vacations or holidays are important for resting weary leaders, daily and weekly "disciplines of replenishment" are the real antidote to stressful living and potential burnout. Without such disciplines in his life, the stressed leader will quickly burn relational bridges, fall subject to anger and emotional swings, lose track of his spiritual moorings, experience health impacts due to excessive stress-related hormones, lose mental focus and clarity, and eventually fail to pay heed to his moral and ethical compass. While you may have your own disciplines of replenishment, here are some which work for me:

Sabbath Rest

For starters, God who created man understands His Creation's need for rest and replenishment. God felt this so important that He instituted a "Sabbath rest" as part of the Ten Commandments:

> "[8] Remember the Sabbath day, to keep it holy. [9] Six days you shall labor and do all your work, [10] but the seventh day is a Sabbath of the LORD your God; *in it you shall not do any work*, you or your son or your daughter, your male or your female servant or your cattle or your sojourner who stays with you."
> (Exodus 20:8-10, underlines added)

I have found that if I don't observe a day of rest each week that I "run out of gas" sometime mid-week and my net output and perspective as a leader are diminished. Certainly busy leaders often have to be creative in observing a Sabbath rest, but this is possible. Wise pastors engaged in a multitude of activities on Sundays often use Monday for this purpose. Military leaders have to navigate the realities of field training and operational deployments which often span over Sundays. Despite these challenges to observing Sabbath rest once a week, the principle remains the same: we as leaders must allow time for ourselves and others to "hit a knee" for rest, reflection, and replenishment across every category of Comprehensive Self-Care™. The alternative is unacceptable.

I recall a story about the Bolsheviks in the early days of the Communist revolution in Russia. Seeking to increase productivity, they adopted a "Continuous Work Week" under Stalin's Five Year Plan, abolishing Sunday as a day of rest and worship. The results were eventually disastrous for the welfare of workers and their families, as well as leading to decreased worker productivity and motivation.

I had the privilege of talking to Pastor Bill Hybels of Willow Creek Community Church at a "Movement Day" Conference in New York City in September 2010. We discussed "life giving leadership" and the importance of understanding how leader energy works. He stated that "the job of leaders is to energize their team toward success" with a key question being, "Who or what should I energize today?" He also emphasized a few of his own disciplines of replenishment to ensure his own leader energy stayed strong.

Work Ending Rituals

One of Bill Hybels' disciplines of replenishment relates to "endings and rituals." Basically, how does one end the work day? His general practice is to schedule a work ending recreational activity with family or friends (sailing in his case) that provides something to look forward to, that curtails the work day, and that helps you forget your "to do" list for a few hours.

In my own case, a "911 Friend" who lives nearby (Mr. Bobby Farino, a realtor, golf professional, and spiritual battle buddy in Williamsburg, VA) is a wonderful social director, often diverting me into a short fishing outing or a few holes of golf at the end of the work day. Reeling in a ferocious six-pound largemouth bass or sinking that winning birdie putt provides great relief from the stresses of a high speed work and travel schedule. While sailing, fishing, or golfing may not be your cup of tea, there are still rituals (recreational or otherwise) to end your day. As a very simple example, what tree do you figuratively hang all your work worries on before you enter the front door of your home? Don't worry; they will still be there when you depart in the morning!

Lowering Ambient Noise

One other discipline of replenishment that Bill Hybels mentioned in our discussion was "lowering the ambient noise of life." This was useful counsel to me, given my predisposition to "multi-task" (work on the computer with TV in background while texting and maybe listening to an MP3 player or chatting with others on phone or in person, all at the same time). Sound familiar? The "noise" of unnecessary sounds, as well as numerous other multi-tasking activities, exacts a significant toll on one's physical, mental, spiritual, emotional, and relational energies.

I have found that actually turning many of these distractions off or down in volume leads to far greater mental focus and emotional sense of well-being. Lowering "ambient noise" can make a big difference in your own self-care. For Bill Hybels' thoughts regarding leader self-care, see Chapter 12 ("Developing an Enduring Spirit") in his book *Courageous Leadership*.

Visualization ("Minute Vacations")

Another useful discipline of replenishment is "minute vacations," the visualization of a positive past experience that incites a relaxation response. In U.S. Army Ranger School, the Ranger cadre teaches the "lock knee" technique of walking up steep inclines. Locking the knee back for a brief moment with each step allows blood to return to the muscles more easily, providing much needed oxygen, and allowing greater leg endurance on a tough climb. In an analogous way, periodic minute vacations allow a relaxation response which enhance one's ability to navigate stress and tough conditions mentally, spiritually, and emotionally, essentially providing "oxygen" to the tired spirit.

An example for me is a minute vacation to the snow skiing paradise in Vail, Colorado. I will picture myself at the top of a Black Diamond slope, smelling the fresh powder from overnight and sensing the cold on my exposed cheeks. Then I visualize beginning to sideslip down the mountain, then a wide traverse observing the valley below, then fall line skiing with all my concentration focused on the next turn and the growing burn in my thighs, and finally the last tuck to cross an imaginary finish line. Of course, the virtual hot chocolate in the warming hut is a final image of comfort not to be overlooked.

Spiritual Meditation

From a more spiritual perspective, meditation upon scripture is powerful for deep relaxation and refilling the well of courage. I have found the following Biblical premise (Isaiah 26:3, Amplified, underlines added) to be an important promise for hard pressed leaders:

> "[3] You will guard him *and* keep him in <u>perfect *and* constant peace whose mind</u> [both its inclination and its character] <u>is stayed on You</u>, because he commits himself to You, leans on You, *and* hopes confidently in You."

Hence, meditation on soothing passages of scripture, as well as music drawn from the Scriptures, can result in a sense of spiritual and emotional wellbeing, and is often "just what the doctor ordered."   Such basic meditation techniques create a relaxation response, allowing for "a minute vacation" in the midst of a demanding workload, or a developing crisis, or relational tensions. Using another analogy, such emotional and spiritual "aerial refueling" is often a lifesaver, sustaining one between times of more extensive refilling of the well of courage (including Sabbath rest mentioned earlier).

In 1996 I was experiencing a significant amount of stress while on temporary duty in England. It was one of those times when I felt like I might "redline" from stress, or even fall into burnout. During a short walk before another demanding day, I stood quietly by the River Thames in London and watched the historic river slowly flow past. Later that same day, I attended a small worship service where "Like a River Glorious" was sung by a dear friend. The intersection of the soothing visual image of the river with this powerful song based on Isaiah 66:12 ("Behold, I extend peace to her like a river...") created a powerful stress relief tool for me which continues to this day. When I need to go to my "happy place," seeing the river in my mind and repeating the words of this well know song are just the right tonic:

> Like a river glorious is God's perfect peace,
> Over all victorious, in its bright increase;
> Perfect, yet it floweth, fuller every day,
> Perfect, yet it groweth, deeper all the way.

Stayed upon Jehovah, hearts are fully blest
Finding, as He promised, perfect peace and rest.
(Chorus, *Like A River Glorious*, Frances R. Havergal, 1876, public domain)

These disciplines of replenishment are useful tools for refreshment and replenishment in the stressful life of a leader. As well, such relaxation techniques are useful for individuals with Posttraumatic Stress symptoms. There are currently several useful mobile "APPS" on the market for PTSD sufferers that lead one through progressive relaxation and visualization exercises, helping them back away from triggers and negative thought patterns.

Sleep Management

Another discipline of replenishment which I benefit from personally is simply sleep management, including power naps. This is extremely important in light of the fact that the brain restores neurotransmitter hormones (serotonin, norepinephrine, and dopamine) during sleep. Physiologically, loss of sleep leads to degraded mental capabilities.

A little lesson in brain chemistry is useful here. In his book *Demystifying Depression: Medical Insights for Hope and Healing*, Dr Greg Knopf, M.D., sheds medical light on our term "well of courage." While I recommend his entire book and the associated website (www.depressionoutreach.com) for a simple and valuable explanation of brain chemistry impact on mental and behavioral health, a couple of short paragraphs have direct applicability to our topic of sleep management:

> "Neurotransmitters are hormones or chemicals that "hand off" or "transmit" the signal from one nerve to another across a gap called the "synapse." There are many neurotransmitters, some of which have not yet been fully identified. These include: Serotonin, Norepinephrine, Acetylcholine and Dopamine."
> (page 11)

As Dr. Knopf continues, he discusses the impacts on brain function:

> "In order to function normally, <u>you need to have a full reservoir</u> (well of courage) or 'tank' of the hormones in the nerve cell ready to be released and 'bridge the gap' (synapse), thus communicating the 'message' to the next nerve. (portions omitted) <u>If there is depletion of the neurotransmitter hormones so that the brain doesn't have an adequate amount in the reservoir, it will begin to malfunction.</u>" (pp 11, 12, parenthetical comment and underlines added)

Now he draws the connection to sleep management:

> "The brain 'fills up' the tanks of serotonin, norepinephrine and dopamine during sleep.

Consequently, <u>if you do not get adequate sleep</u>, you will be starting the next day without a normal reservoir of neurotransmitters, putting you <u>at risk for sub-optimal functioning</u>." (pp 12, 13, underline added)

While this conclusion regarding sleep deprivation may be intuitive, particularly for leaders who tend to burn the candle at both ends, recent medical breakthroughs which allow us to "see" the brain through a variety of new technologies has greatly expanded our understanding of the complex interaction between physical, mental, emotional, relational, and spiritual factors on the brain and the entire body. As noted by Dr. Knopf, sleep and regular exercise both improve brain hormone levels, which in turn improve emotional regulation of conditions such as depression and reactions such as courage. As well, positive spiritual and relational experiences also enhance brain chemistry and overall functioning. While this entire subject is dynamic, fascinating, and very complex, it is undeniable that leaders need sleep, and they must be wise enough to fight for it in the midst of demanding schedules and challenging conditions.

As a young officer I learned from Army sleep deprivation studies that cognitive skills (information tracking, thinking, deciding) degraded far more quickly than physical skills in sleep deprived personnel. Knowing that sleep deprivation affects a leader's core duties more quickly, I recognized the need to be creative about gaining rest.

When I was a company commander at Fort Campbell, I developed the routine (when in a garrison setting) of taking a 15 minute "power nap" during the middle of the day, a powerful way to renew perspective and energy. In an operational setting in the field, I took power naps whenever feasible, including under the extended fuel pods of our Blackhawk command helicopter on a mountain top at the National Training Center, inside field Tactical Operations Centers with generators blaring, and in the seat or cargo hold of many a Humvee. Proper sleep management is critical in continuous field operations or crisis settings where sleep deprivation becomes the norm. Regrettably, the leader suffering from serious sleep deprivation is often the last to recognize the degradation in their performance. Leaders in any domain must fight for rest, an essential way to replenish, to refill their well of courage.

Personal Risk Management™ for Leaders

From a leader self-care perspective, it is certainly important to observe these disciplines of replenishment which reverse the expenditure of courage and energy from your well of courage. It is equally important to be aware of vulnerabilities that might lead to catastrophic moral failure, unwise decisions, or avoidable interpersonal tensions. To manage personal risk, an essential life skill for resilient leaders, the leader must identify the risks in his personal life, put controls in place to mitigate these risks, and stay alert to changing risk factors across all areas of Comprehensive Personal Fitness™.

"HALT"

You may have heard the acronym "HALT" as a caution to leaders, meaning beware of your particular vulnerabilities when "Hungry, Angry, Lonely, or Tired." This useful and simple acronym has been widely applied in addiction recovery, parenting, executive coaching, and spiritual counseling venues.

Leaders should allow "HALT" to inform their situational awareness, prompting them to take caution when "risks" of hunger (and I would add "hurt" to this) anger (and I would add "afraid" to this), loneliness, or fatigue (tiredness) make them vulnerable to undesirable actions or attitudes.

A Biblical example which illustrates "HALT" occurs with the Prophet Elijah. To summarize an action-packed historical account from I Kings 18-20, God sent Elijah to King Ahab, the leader of Israel, because of the severe drought in Samaria. At that time the nation of Israel was following the Gods of Baal, which included the practice of child sacrifice. In fact, Jezebel (the evil and influential wife of King Ahab who encouraged idol worship, wickedness, and sorcery) killed most of the prophets who served the one true God. With the help of Obadiah, the leader of the royal household who had saved 100 of these God fearing prophets from execution,

Elijah confronted King Ahab's failure to embrace the true God of Israel, and challenged the authority of the prophets of Baal, trusting in his Lord God to bring rain to the nation of Israel and save the people from starvation. This "show down" between two competing world views occurred at Mount Carmel in northern Israel and demonstrated the impotence of the prophets of Baal contrasted with the power of Elijah's God who brought fire from Heaven to consume a water-soaked altar. Elijah then directed the execution of the impostors of Baal, prayed for God to bring rain to the land, and once again saw God's power displayed mightily as the sky grew black with clouds and winds, and a heavy shower which ended the drought. Learning of these events, Jezebel then sought to have Elijah killed as well.

With this context, consider these verses from I Kings 19:3-8 (underlines provided for emphasis) which illustrate "HALT" in Elijah's life. First we see that Elijah was understandably afraid, yet he left his servant, went into the desert alone, and succumbed to discouragement to the point of wanting to die. Notably, he was to the point of physical, emotional, and spiritual exhaustion after one of the most significant "victories" of his career (which is often a point of vulnerability for leaders). At this point, he was certainly afraid and angry, lonely (he had isolated himself), and tired (no doubt sleep-deprived, along with other forms of depletion). In short, his well of courage was empty:

> *"³ And <u>he was afraid</u> and arose and ran for his life (because of Jezebel's death threat) and came to Beersheba which belongs to Judah (the nation to the south of Israel in those times), and <u>left his</u>*

servant there. ⁴ But he himself went <u>a day's journey</u>
<u>into the wilderness</u>, and came and sat down under
a juniper tree; and <u>he requested for himself that he</u>
<u>might die</u>, and said, "It is enough; now, O LORD,
take my life, for I am not better than my fathers."

Wisely at this point, Elijah crashed (halted) under a tree, a good first step when "HALT" sets in! Then God provided an angel to remind him to eat, a good second step. Then he rested some more, indicating the state of exhaustion and reminding us that recovery sometimes takes more than just a power nap or minute vacation. No doubt the angel also helped to defeat the loneliness and despair which Elijah was facing, just as close friends who often become "ministering angels" to us in time of need.

"⁵ He <u>lay down and slept</u> under a juniper tree; and
behold, there was an angel touching him, and he
said to him, "<u>Arise, eat</u>." ⁶ Then he looked and
behold, there was at his head a bread cake baked
on hot stones, and a jar of water. <u>So he ate and</u>
<u>drank and lay down again</u>.

After addressing each of his "HALT" vulnerabilities, Elijah then had the strength and motivation to "continue the mission." He moved forward in strength and confidence to his next assignment from God.

"⁷The angel of the LORD came again a second time
and touched him and said, "Arise, eat, because the
journey is too great for you." ⁸ So he arose and ate

and drank, and went in the strength of that food forty days and forty nights to Horeb, the mountain of God."

In summary, "HALT" is a useful tool for leaders, reminding each to recognize our vulnerability when we encounter one or more of the HALT conditions: hungry, angry/afraid, lonely, or tired. And the remedy is often very simple: stop ("HALT"), eat, loosen our grip on anger and fear through communion with God and others (which also defeats our loneliness), and rest. It is amazing how such small adjustments can change our whole physical, mental, spiritual, emotional and relational state of being. As my good friend and respected counselor, Dr. Eric Scalise, would say, "Take the pebble out of your shoe" (alluding to the simple act of removing an obvious irritant or vulnerability and the problem instantly disappears).

"Beware the Bubble"

Although I direct this "Beware the Bubble" caution primarily to senior leaders, the concept applies at every level. It is always a temptation to "lord it over" those below them, embracing an elitist attitude of self-importance. This attitude quickly separates leader from led. "The Bubble" is a danger for all of us.

A certain degree of isolation is inherent with the role of a leader. Particularly with senior leaders, some isolation is necessary to protect their time and energies, as well as their physical security. Senior leaders, however, need to guard against the unwarranted growth of an elitist culture of invulnerability which often blinds them and those in their immediate service to moral temptations and rationalizations. Said more simply, senior leaders need to "Beware the Bubble" that forms around them, isolating them from unvarnished feedback and making them particularly vulnerable to moral excesses. During 2012 in the Army alone, three four-star generals (along with a number of other generals and colonels) all fell victim to poor choices by themselves or by close staff advising them.

The antidote to this bubble phenomenon begins with the leader. A selfless servant-leader who operates from a platform of high personal character will inherently foster similar selflessness and respect for others in those around them, avoiding the narcissistic temptation to think that it is "all about them." This leader also needs to make it very clear to his staff that he will not tolerate a cavalier, elitist approach. The senior leader and supporting personal staff who are trapped in such a bubble often begin to feel that they are above the law, turning a blind eye to standards that others must abide by. Such attitudes often generate overly optimistic assessments which allow the command to be blindsided by reality. Senior leaders must ensure they and their personal staffs are "leaning in the right direction" on such matters, or they are highly vulnerable to a catastrophic fall from grace (referring to our *Resilient Warriors* quote by Archibald Signorelli: "If we yield to evil persuasions, it is because <u>we fall the way we lean</u>, Page 220," underline added).

> A selfless servant-leader who operates from a platform of high personal character will inherently foster similar selflessness and respect for others in those around them, avoiding the narcissistic temptation to think that it is "all about them."

Self-Care Checkup

While a leader may not stop in the middle of a fire fight or a major crisis to assess his level of stress, it does make sense for leaders to be aware of their own stressors that grind away energy, focus, health and Comprehensive Personal Fitness™ in their own lives. Such self-awareness is healthy and essential.

Dr. Eric Scalise, a trusted friend, father of two Marines, experienced mental health professional, and a Vice President of the American Association of Christian Counselors (AACC), is a leading expert on the subject of leader self-care. Dr. Scalise has used his self-care expertise for a number of years with leaders, pastors, and other caregiving professionals. Most recently, I observed Dr. Scalise mentor a group of senior military chaplains who found his material highly relevant in coping with their constant caregiver demands.

See Appendix 1 for a Leader Self-Care Tutorial and Checkup, based upon Dr. Scalise's work.

Gaining Altitude

Self-care is an essential part of resilient leadership. Leaders must "put on their mask first" or they will quickly need help themselves. The first step is a concerted effort toward COMPREHENSIVE SELF-CARE™ across the physical, mental, spiritual, emotional, and relational domains. In addition, there are a number of disciplines of replenishment which help the stressed leader conduct "aerial refueling" to prevent depletion of their well of courage:

- Sabbath Rest

- Work Ending Rituals

- Lowering Ambient Noise

- Visualization

- Spiritual Meditation

- Sleep Management

Self-care also means Personal Risk Management™ to stay out of perceived or real situations which call one's character or reputation into question. Far too often, charismatic and highly competent leaders fall by the wayside because they have given in to personal temptation. Our earlier observation in Chapter 2 that "character always trumps competence" certainly applies here.

Personal Risk Management™, to include awareness of "HALT" and "Beware the Bubble," is an essential skill for resilient leaders.

Resilient Leader Takeaways

RL 61 – The reality is that we all have a reservoir, a well of courage, which is limited in capacity and must be refilled to avoid depletion.

RL 62 – "How do we not grow weary and lose heart as leaders?" is one of the most relevant questions of our time and critical to the subject of resilient leadership. Resilient leaders know how to counteract continual stressors in order to stay in the game.

RL 63 – To help others we must first help ourselves.

RL 64 – The leader competency to offset excessive stress and burnout is "Comprehensive Self-Care™" aimed at continual renewal across the full spectrum of physical, mental, spiritual, emotional, and relational fitness.

RL 65 – While longer periods of rest are important, daily and weekly "disciplines of replenishment" are the real antidote to stressful living and potential burnout.

RL 66 – Sabbath Rest, Work Ending Rituals, Lowering Ambient Noise, Visualization, Spiritual Meditation, and Sleep Management are important techniques of replenishment.

RL 67 – Recent findings regarding brain chemistry reinforce the importance of sleep management to minimize the psychological and physiological impacts of sleep loss.

RL 68 – Personal Risk Management™ is a critical leader skill. "HALT" is a useful acronym to alert leaders to particular vulnerability when they are Hungry, Angry, Lonely, or Tired.

Additional Study

1. Hybels, Bill. *Courageous Leadership*. Grand Rapids, MI: Zondervan, 2002.

2. Internet searches related to leader self-care, stress reduction, and "HALT – Hungry, Angry, Lonely, Tired", (including a sermon by Dr Charles Stanley at http://jesuslovesmethisiknow.com/index79.html and a helpful Catholic blog which also highlights HALT at http://bustedhalo.com/features/what-works-10-halt-hungry-angry-lonely-tired)

3. Hart, Archibald. *The Hidden Link between Adrenaline and Stress*. Waco, TX: Word Publishing, 1986.

4. Cloud, Henry and John Townsend. *Boundaries*. Grand Rapids, MI: Zondervan Publishing House, 1992.

5. Swenson, Richard A. *Margin: Restoring Emotional, Physical, Financial, and Time Reserves To Overloaded Lives.* Colorado Springs, CO: NavPress, 1992.

6. Knopf, Gregory. *Demystifying Depression.* Portland, OR: In the Light Communications, 2009.

9

Follow Me!
The Ultimate Resilient Leader

"The U.S. Army Infantry Motto, 'Follow Me' was adopted as a result of the rallying cry of Colonel Aubry S. 'Red' Newman, Commander, 34th Infantry Regiment, during the beach assault at Leyte.

He stood up in the midst of menacing Japanese gunfire and said, 'get the hell off the beach. Get up and get moving. <u>Follow Me</u>.' He then led his troops forward in attack."

As a "wet behind the ears" second lieutenant reporting for the Infantry Officer Basic Course at Fort Benning, Georgia in 1972,

I soon found myself in front of Infantry Hall looking up into the eyes of a large sculpture called, "Follow Me." The bigger-than-life replica (over ten feet tall) of an impressive infantryman (fashioned in 1960 after a model Army Infantryman named Eugene J. Wyles) shows this infantry leader with his right hand thrust forward in the air, making the infantry hand and arm signal to "Follow Me." In one brief encounter with "Iron Mike" (the nickname the statue acquired over the years), I was reminded of the essence of leadership and soldiering on any battlefield in the military or beyond. Throughout a military career in the Infantry, I traveled and studied many times at Fort Benning, always hearing the echoes of many great leaders who had gone before, leaders who had bravely said "Follow Me" at the risk of their very lives, to point the way for others. I studied their characteristics diligently, seeking to emulate their best qualities on behalf of those under my leadership.

Another great leader, Jesus, also gave the command "Follow Me," recorded in the Gospel of Matthew. For context, before Jesus gave this command to "Follow Me," He had been baptized by John, approved by God, guided by the Spirit into the wilderness, fasted for forty days and forty nights, and tempted by Satan with the lust of the flesh, and the lust of the eyes, and the pride of life (as we discussed earlier in Chapter 7, "HALT"). He proved Himself faithful even under the most intense of temptation and harsh conditions, and was fully prepared to lead others in His earthly ministry. After all this, He began His life of leadership by simply directing "Follow Me."

> *"Now when Jesus was walking by the Sea of Galilee, He saw two brothers, Simon who was called Peter, and Andrew his brother, casting a net into the sea; for they were fishermen. And He said to them 'Follow Me, and I will make you fishers of men.' Immediately they left their nets and followed Him."* (Matthew 4:18-20, underlines added)

This is how Jesus of Galilee, the Ultimate Resilient Leader, modeled leadership at the beginning of His adult ministry. He led by example, from the front, not asking His followers to do anything He would not do. He simply said, "Follow Me."

As a leadership bookend at the end of His earthly presence, the resurrected Jesus reemphasized "Follow Me" as He gave final direction to His disciples before His ascension to Heaven. You have already heard about the great fishing story in John 21, from which we drew the "Do your troops know that you need them?" acid test of leadership (Chapter 7). After Jesus said, "Bring some of the fish which you have now caught," He followed with, "Come and have breakfast." Then He engaged in several final dialogs with Peter, who was soon to transition from a coarse fisherman to the strong leader of the first century church. Throughout His life as a leader, Jesus practiced what today we would call "leader development," consistently investing in the growth of others.

Shepherd My Sheep

The first dialog between Peter and Jesus deals with the commitment of a leader, and cuts to the heart of servant leadership. Jesus asks Peter if he loves Him, using the word *agape* (Greek, representing the purest and most selfless form of love). Peter responds with a lower expression of love in the form of *phileo* (Greek, brotherly love). Jesus then directs him to "Tend My lambs." This exchange repeats itself with Jesus concluding, "Shepherd My sheep" (a higher degree of leader responsibility and selflessness). A third iteration of this dialog ensues with Peter finally responding with the higher form of love (*agape*) which Jesus had used, demonstrating the greatest possible commitment to Jesus as a person and leader. Jesus then reiterates a simple instruction to this emerging servant leader, "Tend My sheep."

While this rich passage in John 21 lends itself to many important themes across a wide spectrum of application, we as leaders must not miss its linkage to our definition of leadership drawn from Psalm 78:72 (Chapter 1):

> *"So he <u>shepherded</u> them* (selfless service) *according to the integrity of his heart* (character), *and guided them with his skillful hands* (competence)." (parenthetical comments and underline added)

Nor should we miss the direct connection to our first two acid tests of leadership in Chapter 5: "Do your troops know your voice in the dark?" and "Do you know your troops?" both of which we drew from John 10. As well, John 10 highlights "they follow me" as the end state of such leadership. In the words of Jesus,

> "My sheep <u>hear my voice</u>,
> and <u>I know them</u>,
> and they <u>follow me</u>."
> (John 10:27, underlines added)

One additional point about love and leadership in our John 21 discussion between Jesus and Peter: leadership is highly relational and ultimately about love in its highest form (*agape*). As we shepherd (lead) others, we must ask if we love our followers enough to help them achieve God's full potential for their lives, or if we love them enough to give them the joy and affirmation of accomplishing something bigger than themselves, or if we love enough to help them navigate the darkest hours of trauma and suffering, or if we love them to the degree of sacrificing our own comfort on their behalf. Just as pure and undefiled religion is a love relationship with the person of Jesus, so ultimately leadership is a relationship of sacrificial love between the leader and the led.

Even the crustiest of Marine gunnery sergeants, profit-focused business executives, process-focused engineers, hard-charging coaches and teachers, and performance-oriented parents must recognize these relational dynamics in order to be fully effective as leaders.

You Follow Me!

The second leadership dialog in the closing chapter of John continues the "Follow Me" theme. Immediately following the shepherding discussion, Jesus dives deeper with Peter, discussing the manner in which Peter will die ("someone else will gird you, and bring you where you do not wish to go," alluding to Peter's eventual death by crucifixion as well). Rather than dwelling on the pathos of Peter's death, Jesus returns immediately to the simple instruction, "Follow Me." This was no doubt a powerful reminder from three short years prior when after the same command Peter and Andrew had "left their nets and followed Him." Now, as Jesus is sending them off to be leaders under the most challenging conditions, He simply reiterates, "Follow Me." Essentially, Jesus is reminding them of their call, their purpose, and their mission. As you may recall from the pages of *Resilient Warriors* (pages 85-88), this emphasis on "Calling" is important in the before, during, and after of individual resilience. Here we are reminded it is also a leader responsibility to draw their people and their organization back to the high and noble calling for which they serve.

Peter, characteristically curious about what would happen to the disciple John, questions Jesus, *"Lord, and what about this man?"* Jesus basically tells Peter to "work his own lane" by saying,

"If I want him to remain until I come, what is that to you? You "follow Me!" (John 21:21-22)

In the world of leadership, it is critical to "keep the main thing, the main thing." Despite many detractors around us, we must continue to follow the prime example of Jesus and other leadership role models by not getting derailed by other things. In this vein, the first four verses of Hebrews 12 (introduced in Chapter 8) are worth restating:

> "[1]Therefore, since we have so great a cloud of witnesses surrounding us, let us also lay aside every encumbrance and the sin which so easily entangles us, and let us run with endurance the race that is set before us, [2] fixing our eyes on Jesus, the author and perfecter of faith, who for the joy set before Him endured the cross, despising the shame, and has sat down at the right hand of the throne of God. [3] For consider Him who has endured such hostility by sinners against Himself, so that you will not grow weary and lose heart."
> (Hebrews 12:1-3, underlines added)

Fix our eyes on Jesus, the Ultimate Resilient Leader.

Consider Him, the Ultimate Resilient Leader.

Gaining Altitude

Let's ensure that we don't miss the forest for the trees. Certainly *Resilient Leaders* discusses many useful leadership techniques and strategies. Certainly the stories are interesting and relevant. Certainly the character sketches are instructive. Certainly we are struck by the leadership wisdom to be gleaned from the pages of the Bible. But, let us not miss the best part. Whether you think Jesus was merely a great person and prophet, or you are a true follower of Christ, one cannot address the full spectrum of leadership without paying close attention to the person of Jesus, along with the spiritual wellbeing of those they lead.

> Whether you think Jesus was merely a great person and prophet, or you are a true follower of Christ, one cannot address the full spectrum of leadership without paying close attention to the person of Jesus...

For Christ followers, this means embracing not only the principles of Jesus, but also the person and the power of Jesus as we lead others. Jesus demonstrated the greatest resilience in all history, literally falling from the Cross (crucifixion) into a cold tomb and the abyss of hell, and bouncing back to life (resurrection) to appear on earth and ascend to the right hand of God the Father. From there He intercedes for each of us daily. He was "beaten down, but not destroyed," bouncing higher than ever before.

Jesus captures it well when He highlights the believer's dependence upon Him, the true source of strength, significance, and success of all people, including leaders:

"⁵ I am the vine, you are the branches; he who abides in Me and
I in him,
he bears much fruit, <u>for apart from Me you can do nothing</u>."
(John 15:5, underlining added)

In *Resilient Leaders*, we have only illumined a small portion of the leadership life of Jesus which was recorded in the Bible, much less the totality of His life which was never fully recorded. As John writes in the last verse of his Gospel, "there were also many other things which Jesus did, which if they were written in detail, I suppose that <u>even the world itself would not contain the books that would be written</u>." (John 21:25, underline added) The purpose here is to jumpstart your own continued investigation of Jesus as the Ultimate Resilient Leader. Whatever your crucible of leadership might hold in coming days, may you continue to grow in leadership character and competence as you mine golden leadership nuggets from the life of Jesus.

Similarly, the totality of the Bible is packed with priceless leadership gems. It is the world's best leadership manual. Reinforcing Jesus' theme of dependence on Him, the book of Wisdom (Proverbs) likewise places the role of the leader in proper perspective. Certainly leaders must be diligent to do everything possible to "set the conditions" for success of their organization; but ultimately leaders must recognize their dependence on a sovereign God:

"³¹ The horse is prepared for the day of battle,
but <u>victory belongs to the LORD</u>."
(Proverbs 21:31, underline added)

One more example which highlights a leader's dependency upon the Lord comes from the pages of Psalms:

> "¹Unless the LORD builds the house,
> They labor in vain who build it;
> Unless the LORD guards the city,
> The watchman keeps awake in vain."
> (Psalm 127:1, underlines added)

A personal vignette further emphasizes the central tenet that the leader who depends upon spiritual power beyond self is able to tap the full potential within him and those he leads:

While in the middle of the mountain phase of Ranger School in December 1972 (you recall earlier accounts of the severe winter conditions that year in the mountains of north Georgia), Ranger Dees begrudgingly went on "sick call" for a worsening respiratory condition. The cadre transported me to a doctor in a local community who x-rayed me and concluded that I had pneumonia in one lung. After the cold and bumpy ride back to the Ranger camp, I was informed that I would be out-processed the next day, sent home packing like so many others with injuries and serious medical conditions. Admittedly discouraged about not making the cut in Ranger school, I remember spending the somewhat sleepless night in soul searching and prayer. I don't remember any blinding flashes from God, but the next morning I felt compelled to jump back on the sick call truck (with considerable "guff" from the cadre) to revisit the doctor in town. His second x-ray indicated that my lung was now clear of infection, a very graphic picture when placed next to the previous day's x-ray showing significant fluids and infection in the lung. As with a blind man who Jesus healed ("one thing I do know that though I was blind, now I see." John 9:25), I couldn't explain medically or spiritually what had occurred. I did know, however, that God in some way had provided a new lease on life in Ranger school.

Characteristic of challenging training such as Ranger school, the cadre chose to insert me back into the ongoing field operation in a realistic way. After reuniting with my rucksack and other field gear, I was taken to an isolated road intersection and left to wait, for minutes, then hours until it became dark and even colder. Unexpectedly, a group of Viet Cong role players in black pajamas and pointed straw hats arrived in an Army "deuce and a half" truck (2.5 ton capacity). Blinded by the lights, I quickly found myself surrounded by these enemy role players who stuffed me in a jeep with "opposing force" markings. Apparently, I was now their Prisoner of War (POW). They began to move slowly down the county road with foot soldiers moving in front and behind of the jeep where I was held captive, soon diverting onto a small dirt trail through the middle of the woods.

All of a sudden, all hell broke loose. Flash grenades, machine gun fire to the front and rear of the column, people diving into any crevice which might protect them, leaders shouting instructions, totally chaotic. My "Viet Cong" driver and body guards jumped out of the jeep to fight the ambush. Seeing my chance, I jumped out of the jeep and tried to orient myself.

Suddenly, a voice from the dark:

"Bob, is that you?" shouted out Ranger Chuck Drobny (one of my West Point classmates who remains a close friend, and has become a very successful resilient leader and man of God).

I knew the voice in the dark immediately, "Yea, Chuck ... it's me!"

Unbeknownst to me, I was the object of a "POW Snatch" mission conducted by the Ranger platoon to which I was assigned, comprised of many West Point classmates who I had bonded with over our four years at the Military Academy. They had freed me from the enemy patrol, literally rescuing me from darkness and captivity and transferring me back into a world of friends, and safety, and purpose. Our missions continued from there.

This profound metaphor regarding the work of Jesus Christ, the Ultimate Resilient Leader, was too powerful to miss. Just as my Ranger comrades had freed me from the enemy captors, so Jesus had also freed me from an even more powerful and real enemy. The Ranger experience was short term training while the work of Jesus in my life, and in the lives of other believers, is the real deal, for a lifetime and beyond. As it records in the book of Colossians:

"¹³ For He rescued us from the domain of darkness,
and transferred us to the kingdom of His beloved Son,
¹⁴ in whom we have redemption, the forgiveness of sins."
(Colossians 3:13-14, underlines added)

Not only can leaders have redemption and forgiveness of sins through the person of Jesus, they can also have the "secret sauce" of leadership which affords them unmatched resources to lead selflessly with character and competence, to lead with resilience over time, and to lead from a position of dependence, devotion, and direction which is rooted in the Creator God Himself.

Jesus truly was the Ultimate Resilient Leader. We do well to follow Him.

Landing the Plane

In *Resilient Leaders* we have together looked at leadership through a Biblical lens, recognizing the Bible as the world's greatest leadership manual and Jesus as the world's greatest leadership role model, the Ultimate Resilient Leader. Drawing our basic definition of leadership from the life of David in Psalm 78, "*So he shepherded them* (selfless service) *according to the integrity of his heart* (character), *and guided them with his skillful hands* (competence)," we acknowledged the importance of "selfless service over time from a platform of character and competence." After exposing the "rough and tumble" realities of leadership, we dove deeply into the essence of leader character, focusing on Selflessness, Integrity, Courage, and Wisdom. We then dissected resilient leader competencies, using our Resilience Life Cycle© Before, During, and After model from *Resilient Warriors*. After a sober look at the real potential of leader burnout, we addressed the important discipline of Leader Self-Care, and closed with a final focus on Jesus as the Ultimate Resilient Leader.

In the course of this *Resilient Leaders* journey, we also offered three acid tests of leadership:

- ***Do your troops know your voice in the dark?***

- ***Do you know your troops?***

- ***Do your troops know that you need them?***

As I noted in our introductory chapter, there are many great leadership books on the market. I have recommended many in our Additional Study sections within each chapter. I have not attempted to replicate the multitude of leadership principles found in these other books. Rather, I have focused on the life stories and leadership lessons which God burned deeply into me as father and husband, military professional, business executive, non-profit leader, community activist on behalf of the military, and as a follower of Jesus.

Prayerfully, I have written the book that God wanted me to write, the book that I wish I had as a young leader and throughout my lifetime in the crucibles of guiding and serving others.

Prayerfully, you have heard the messages, the methods, and the motivation which God wanted you to hear.

Now it is time for each of us as resilient leaders to lead from the front as we pursue "excellence *over time* through the realities of success and failure in the tough marketplaces of life."

As you "move out and draw fire" in future crucibles of life and leadership, may you know with certainty that God truly is your

Rock, Fortress, and Deliverer (RFD). In the final analysis, it is the RFD factor that makes a leader resilient.

"The LORD is my rock and my fortress and my deliverer."
(Psalm 18:2b)

Resilient Leader Takeaways

RL 69 – Jesus led by example, from the front, not asking His followers to do anything He would not do.

RL 70 – Throughout His life as a leader, Jesus practiced what today we would call "leader development," consistently investing in the growth of others.

RL 71 – Leadership is highly relational and ultimately about sacrificial love between leader and led.

RL 72 – As modeled by Jesus, a leader must draw others back to the high and noble calling for which they serve.

RL 73 – Leaders must continue to follow the prime example of Jesus and other leadership role models without getting derailed by other things.

RL 74 – Whether you think Jesus was merely a great person and prophet, or you are a true follower of Christ; one cannot address the full spectrum of leadership without paying close attention to the person of Jesus, along with the spiritual wellbeing of those they lead.

RL 75 – The Bible is the world's greatest leadership manual.

RL 76 – Jesus was the Ultimate Resilient Leader. Focus on Him. Consider Him. Follow Him.

Additional Study

1. Blanchard, Ken, and Hodges, Phil. *Lead Like Jesus*. Nashville, TN: Thomas Nelson, 2005.

2. Howlett III, H.C. *Trustworthy Leaders*. Pocatello, ID: TechStar Training, 2007.

3. Briner, Bob, and Pritchard, Ray. *Leadership Lessons of Jesus*. New York, NY: Random House, 1998.

Acknowledgements

As we quoted John Wooden in Chapter 5,

"Life Is A United Effort of Many."

So it has been with this *Resilient Leaders* project. I am very appreciative of the many that have made this *Resilient Leaders* effort such a productive journey.

My beloved wife Kathleen has been the perfect helpmate, consistently sacrificing time and energy to create a work of value for others while she concurrently "kept the home fires burning" for family and friends. As I reflected in *Resilient Warriors*, still waters run deep, and Kathleen's wise insights along the way have been invaluable. As my bride for 39 years, she has been a wonderful life partner, mother, grandmother, and friend. She has modeled resilience many times over, such as moving us 23 times in 31 years during our military service. She no doubt learned this from her highly resilient father and mother,

Charlie and Bobbie Sue Robinson, who have been my greatest cheerleaders over many life endeavors.

Another source of wisdom, encouragement, and tangible assistance has been our dear circle of "911 friends" and family, role models and wise counselors such as: Drs. Andy and Gail Seidel, Dr. Jim and Mary Syvrud, Bobby and Kandy Farino, Ron and Cristy Varela, Gene and Randi Frazier, Jim and Brenda Johnson, Pastor Bill and Lindy Warrick of Williamsburg Community Chapel, Jeff and Karen Koob, Dr. Colonel (Chaplain) Ron Huggler and Colonel Sue Huggler, U.S. Army, Retired, Dr. Eric and Donna Scalise, Dr. LuAnn Callaway, Chuck and Sharron Allen, Bobbie Sue Robinson, Charles and Nancy Robinson, and our beloved children, Major Rob Dees and Allison Dees Barry, along with their respective families.

Our "Resilience God Style" Vine Life Class from Williamsburg Community Chapel provided wonderful friendship and encouragement during the last days of this effort. As well, I am grateful to the New Canaan Society and the American Association of Christian Counselors for the opportunities to present emerging *Resilient Leaders* content in a variety of venues, affording valuable feedback and refinement of the material.

Glen Aubrey of Creative Team Publishing (CTP) (www.CreativeTeamPublishing.com) has been an outstanding editor, publisher, and friend. Justin Aubrey's artistic giftedness was indispensable to the cover designs. The CTP editing team masterfully prepared the final manuscript for publication. Randy Beck of My Domain Tools (www.MyDomainTools.com) did a great job of expanding the *Resilience Trilogy* website (www.ResilienceTrilogy.com), and provided marketing collateral for new content. As well, Rachel Carawan has been a wonderful assistant, untiringly moving forward with research and securing permissions from many contributing organizations and individuals. She has become a valuable member of *The Resilience Trilogy* team.

Foundational to my appreciation and understanding of resilient leadership have been the inspiring leaders and mentors I was privileged to serve under while in the military, business, and non-profit sectors. I am forever indebted to the many I have named in *Resilient Leaders*.

Most importantly, God truly is my Rock, Fortress, and Deliver ("RFD"). Without the friendship of Jesus, the comfort of His Holy Spirit, the wisdom of His Word, and the Sovereign and Sufficient Hand of God the Father, my efforts would only be clanging cymbals and tinkling brass. To Him Be the Glory!

About the Author

ROBERT F. DEES
Major General, U.S. Army, Retired

Major General (Retired) Robert F. Dees was born in Amarillo, Texas on 2 February 1950. Graduating from the US Military Academy in 1972, he was commissioned as a second lieutenant of Infantry and awarded a Bachelor of Science degree. He also holds a Masters degree in Operations Research from the Naval Postgraduate School. His military education includes the Infantry Officer Basic and Advanced Courses, the US Army Command and General Staff College, and the Industrial College of the Armed Forces. He was also a Research Fellow at the Royal College of Defence Studies in London and is a registered Professional Engineer in the State of Virginia.

General Dees served in a wide variety of command and staff positions culminating in his last three assignments as Assistant Division Commander for Operations, 101st Airborne Division (Air Assault); Commander, Second Infantry Division, United States

Forces Korea; and as Deputy Commanding General, V (US/GE) Corps in Europe, concurrently serving as Commander, US-Israeli Combined Task Force for Missile Defense. He commanded airborne, air assault, and mechanized infantry forces from platoon through division level; including two tours as company commander and regimental commander in the historic "Rakkasans," the 187th Regimental Combat Team. General Dees is a Distinguished Member of the Regiment, and now serves as Honorary Colonel of the Regiment for the Rakkasans.

General Dees' awards and decorations include the Defense Distinguished Service Medal, Distinguished Service Medal (2), Legion of Merit (2), Meritorious Service Medal (6), Joint Service Commendation Medal, Army Commendation Medal, and the Republic of Korea Chonsu Order of National Security. General Dees has also been awarded the Ranger Tab, Senior Parachutist and Air Assault Badges, the Expert Infantryman's Badge, the Army Staff Identification Badge, and the Joint Staff Identification Badge. General Dees was also awarded the 2003 Centurion Award by the National Association for Evangelicals for long term support to chaplains while in command positions.

Officially retiring from the Army on 1 January 2003, he worked as Director of Homeland Security for Electronic Warfare Associates; then as Executive Director, Defense Strategies, Microsoft Corporation for two years. In that role, General Dees formulated the strategy for Microsoft's US Defense sector and engaged with leadership of Microsoft's major defense partners. In addition, he served as Microsoft lead for Reconstruction of Iraq, coordinating efforts with US Government, foreign governments, and private sector partners in the US and abroad. General Dees then served for five years (2005-2010) as Executive Director, Military Ministry providing spiritual nurture to troops and families around the world. He is now President of RFD, LLC, serving a variety of constituents in the arenas of business, defense, counterterrorism, and care for military troops and families.

As well, General Dees now serves as Associate Vice President for Military Outreach for Liberty University (leading the Liberty University Institute for Military Resilience), Military Director for the American Association of Christian Counselors, and Senior Military Advisor for DNA Military. He also serves on a number of non-profit boards including Military Community Youth Ministries, Operation Military Family, Hope for the Home Front, and the Invictus Foundation.

General Dees frequently provides motivational talks at a variety of seminars, webinars, and conferences; as well as commentary on current military and combat trauma issues in venues such as FOX Huckabee, FOX Business, Focus on the Family, Christian Broadcasting Network, American Association of Christian Counselors, American Family Radio, New Canaan Society, Pinnacle Forum, Wallbuilders Live, Iron Sharpens Iron Men's Conferences, Wildfire Men's Conferences, and numerous churches and military bases. He was featured as one of thirty "*Master Leaders*" by George Barna.

General Dees is married to the former Kathleen Robinson of Houston, Texas. They have two married children and five grandchildren, and currently live in Williamsburg, Virginia. General and Mrs. Dees are grateful for the privilege of continuing to serve our nation during these critical times.

Permissions and Credits
In Order of Appearance:

Grateful acknowledgement is made to the following for permission to cite previously published material, quotes, and concepts:

Teddy Roosevelt poem "Man in the Arena" excerpted from the speech "Citizenship In A Republic" delivered at the Sorbonne, in Paris, France on 23 April, 1910. Held within the public domain. http://www.theodore-roosevelt.com/trsorbonnespeech.html

Saint Francis of Assisi for the quote "Above all the grace and gifts that Christ gives to His beloved is that of overcoming self." Held within the public domain.

Thomas Nelson, Inc. for excerpts from *Talent is never Enough: Discover the Choices that Will Take You Beyond Your Talent* by John C. Maxwell. Copyright © 2007 by John C. Maxwell. Used by permission of Thomas Nelson, Inc. Nashville TN. All rights reserved.

Pastor Bill Hybels for a sidebar discussion related to leadership. Movement Day Conference, New York, NY. September, 2010.

Dr. Gregory Knopf for quotes from *Demystifying Depression for Christians: Medical Insights for Hope and Healing* by Dr. Gregory Knopf, M.D. Copyright © 2009, 2011 Gregory Knopf, M.D. Used by permission. All rights reserved.

Victory Division for quote found at http://24thid.tripod.com/.

Dr. Eric Scalise for content regarding stress management entitled *Burn out, Stress and Compassion Fatigue: Managing Yourself* from a co-presentation at AACC conference, Branson, MO, October 2011.

Bibliography

An Encyclopedia Britannica Company: Merriam-Webster. 2013. Accessed 2012. http://www.merriam-webster.com.

Armerding, Hudson T. *The Heart of Godly Leadership.* Wheaton, IL: Crossway Books, 1992.

Armerding, Hudson T. *A Word to the Wise.* Wheaton, IL: Tyndale House, 1980.

Aubrey, Glen. *Lincoln, Leadership and Gettysburg: Defining Moments of Greatness.* San Diego: Creative Team Publishing, 2009.

Augustine, Norman R. *Augustine's Laws.* New York: Penguin Books, 1986.

Barna, George. *Master Leaders: Revealing Conversations With 30 Leadership Greats.* With Bill Dallas. Wheaton, IL: BarnaBooks / Tyndale House, 2009.

Batterson, Mark. *In a Pit With a Lion On a Snowy Day: How to Survive and Thrive When Opportunity Roars.* Sisters, Oregon: Multnomah, 2006.

Bennis, Warren and Burt Nanus. *Leaders: The Strategies for Taking Charge.* New York: Perennial Library / Harper & Row, 1986.

Blanchard, Ken and Phil Hodges. *Lead Like Jesus: Lessons from the Greatest Leadership Role Model of All Time.* Nashville: W Publishing Group, 2005.

Bossidy, Larry and Ram Charan. *Execution: The Discipline of Getting Things Done.* With Charles Burck. Revised ed. New York, NY: Crown Business, 2009.

Bright, Bill. *First Love: Renewing Your Passion for God.* Bill Bright Signature Series. Peachtree City, GA: New Life, 2004.

Briner, Bob and Ray Pritchard. *Leadership Lessons of Jesus: Timeless Wisdom for Leaders in Today's World.* New York: Gramercy Books, 1998.

Briner, Bob. *The Management Methods of Jesus: Ancient Wisdom for Modern Business.* Nashville: Nelson Business, 1996.

Buckingham, Clay T. *Nuggets of Gold: Genesis through Malachi.* Self-published without copyright, 2011.

"Bugle Notes: Learn This". *United States Military Academy: West Point.* Accessed July 2012. http://www.west-point.org/academy/malowa/inspirations/ buglenotes.html.

"Cadet Prayer". *United States Military Academy West Point.* Accessed August 2012. http://www.usma.edu/chaplain/SitePages/ Cadet%20Prayer.aspx

Callaway, Sid. *Leadership Lessons for Coaches.* Camby, IN: Power, 2009.

Carawan, Rolfe. *Profiles In Character.* Federal Way, WA: Life Matters, 1996.

Clinton, J. Robert. *The Making of a Leader: Recognizing the Lessons and Stages of Leadership Development.* Colorado Springs, CO: NavPress, 1988.

Cloud, Henry and John Townsend. *Boundaries.* Grand Rapids, Michigan: Zondervan Publishing House, 1992.

Collins, James C. and Jerry I. Porras. *Built to Last: Successful Habits of Visionary Companies.* New York, NY: Harper Business, 1994.

Collins, Jim. *Good to Great: Why Some Companies Make the Leap . . . and Others Don't.* New York: Harper Business, 2001.

Conlon, Carter. *Fear Not.* Ventura, California, USA: Regal, 2012.

Covey, Stephen R. *Principle-Centered Leadership.* 1st Fireside ed. New York: Simon & Schuster, 1991.

Covey, Stephen R. *The 7 Habits of Highly Effective People: Restoring the Character Ethic.* New York: Simon & Schuster, 1989.

Covey, Stephen R., A. Roger Merrill and Rebecca R. Merrill. *First Things First: To Live, to Love, to Learn, to Leave a Legacy.* 1st Fireside ed. New York, NY: Simon & Schuster, 1995.

Crocker III, H. W. *Robert E. Lee On Leadership: Executive Lessons in Character, Courage, and Vision.* Rocklin, CA: FORUM / Prima, 1999.

Dees, Robert F. *Resilient Warriors*. San Diego: Creative Team Publishing, 2011.

---. *Resilient Warriors Advanced Study Guide*. San Diego: Creative Team Publishing, 2012.

---. "Battle Rhythm." *Military Review*, April 1987, pp 59-64.

Department of Defense. "Senior Level Leadership: A Selected Bibliography." Memorandum. Carlisle Barracks, PA: US Army War College, 1982.

Department of the Army. "Leadership and Command at Senior Levels." Army Field Manual No 22-103. Washington, DC: Department of the Army Headquarters, 1987.

Donnithorne, Larry R. *The West Point Way of Leadership: From Learning Principled Leadership to Practicing It*. New York: Currency / Doubleday, 1993.

Dungy, Tony. *Uncommon*. Winter Park, FL: Tyndale, 2009

Fitton, Robert A., comp. *Leadership: Quotations from the World's Greatest Motivators*. Boulder, CO: Westview, 1997.

Fitton, Robert A., ed. *Leadership: Quotations from the Military Tradition*. Boulder, CO: Westview, 1990.

Foth, Dick and Ruth. *When The Giant Lies Down*. Wheaton, IL: Victor Books, 1995.

Foss, Clive. "Stalin's Topsy-Turvy Work Week". *History Today,* 54 (9). 2004. Accessed August 2012. http://www.historytoday.com/clive-foss/stalins-topsy-turvy-work-week

Gladwell, Malcolm. *The Tipping Point: How Little Things Can Make a Big Difference.* Boston: Back Bay Books, 2002. First published 2000 by Little, Brown.

Gongwer, Todd G. *LEAD...for God's Sake!* Carol Stream, IL: Tyndale House Publishers, Inc., 2011.

Hart, Dr. Archibald. *Coping with Depression in the Ministry and Other Helping Professions.* Waco, TX: Word Books, 1984.

---. "Depressed, Stressed, and Burned Out: What's Going on in My Life?" *Enrichment Journal.* Accessed, 2012. http://enrichmentjournal.ag.org/200603/200603_020_burnout.cfm

---. *Hidden Link Between Adrenaline and Stress* . Waco, TX: Word Publishing, 1986.

Hendricks, Howard. "Biblical Ethics for Business Leaders." Lecture given at The Leader Board II Conference, Dallas Theological Seminary, Dallas, TX, May 3, 2004. Compact disc recording.

Hidalgo, C. C. "Definition of Integrity". *Webweevers.* December 16, 2002. Accessed September 2012. http://webweevers.com/integrity/#.UPimVSfLSa9

Hillman, O. S. *Change Agent: Engaging Your Passion to Be the One Who Makes a Difference.* Lake Mary, FL: Charisma House, 2011.

Hodges, Frederick B. "Training For Uncertainty." Monograph. Fort Leavenworth, KS: School of Advanced Military Studies, 1993.

Howlett, H.C. *Trustworthy Leaders.* Pocatello: TECHSTAR, Inc., 2007.

"Hungry-Angry-Lonely-Tired". *Jesus Loves Me This I Know.* Accessed August 2012. http://jesuslovesmethisiknow.cm/index79.html

Hybels, Bill. *Courageous Leadership.* Grand Rapids, MI: Zondervan, 2002

Johnson, Dwight L. *The Transparent Leader: Spiritual Secrets of Nineteen Successful Men.* With Dean Nelson. Mechanicsburg, PA: Executive Books, 2001.

Irwin, Tim. *Run with the Bulls without Getting Trampled.* Nashville, TN: Thomas Nelson, 2006.

Kaplan, Burton. *Strategic Communication: The Art of Making Your Ideas Their Ideas.* New York: Harper Business, 1991.

Kennedy, John F. "Inagural Address, 20 January 1961." *John F. Kennedy Presidential Library and Museum.* Accessed 2012. http://www.jfklibrary.org/Asset-viewer/BqXIEM9F4024ntFl7SVAjA.aspx?gclid=CPqBksalyLICF aY7Ogod_GIAHw

Kolditz, Thomas A. *In Extremis Leadership: Leading as if Your Life Depended On It.* San Francisco, CA: Jossey-Bass, 2007.

Knopf, Dr. Gregory. *Demystifying Depression for Christians: Medical Insights for Hope and Healing.* Portland: In The Light Communications, 2009.

Lee, Gus. *Courage: The Backbone of Leadership.* With Diane Elliot Lee. San Francisco, CA: Jossey-Bass, 2006.

Lee, Eloise. "Here's The Chilling Letter General Eisenhower Drafted In Case The Nazis Won On D-Day." *Business Insider: Military & Defense.* June 6, 2012. Accessed July 2012. http://www.businessinsider.com/d-day-incase-of-failure-letter-by-general-eisenhower-2012-6#ixzz29DzmJVME

Lencioni, Patrick. *The Five Dysfunctions of a Team: A Leadership Fable.* San Francisco: Jossey-Bass, 2002.

Lockerbie, D. Bruce. *A Man Under Orders: Lieutenant General William K. Harrison, Jr.* San Francisco: Harper & Row, 1979.

Loritts Jr., Crawford W. *Leadership as an Identity.* Chicago: Moody, 2009.

Maxwell, John C. *Leadership Gold.* Nashville: Thomas Nelson, 2008.

---. *Talent Is Never Enough: Discover the Choices that Will Take You Beyond Your Talent.* Nashville: Thomas Nelson, 2007.

---. *The 21 Irrefutable Laws of Leadership: Follow Them and People Will Follow You.* Nashville: Thomas Nelson, 1998.

"Medal of Honor Recipients: Korean War". *U.S. Army Center Of Military History*. January 5, 2012. Accessed July 2012. http://www.history.army.mil/html/moh/koreanwar.html

Metaxas, Eric. *Amazing Grace: William Wilberforce and the Heroic Campaign to End Slavery*. New York: Harper Collins, 2007.

———. *Bonhoffer: Pastor, Martyr, Prophet, Spy*. Nashville, TN: Thomas Nelson, 2010.

Moore, Lt. Gen. Harold G. and Joseph L. Galloway. *We Were Soldiers Once... and Young: Ia Drang—the Battle That Changed the War in Vietnam*. New York: Random House, 1992

Moen, Skip. *Word to Lead By: A Practical Daily Devotional on Leading Like Jesus*. Tulsa, OK: Insight, 2005.

Nanus, Burt. *The Leader's Edge: The Seven Keys to Leadership in a Turbulent World*. Chicago: Contemporary Books, 1989.

———. *Visionary Leadership: Creating a Compelling Sense of Direction for Your Organization*. San Francisco: Jossey-Bass, 1992.

Neven, Tom. *On the Frontier: A Personal Guidebook for the Physical, Emotional, and Spiritual Challenges of Military Life*. Colorado Springs, CO: WaterBrook, 2006.

Nimitz, Admiral Chester. *Reflections on Pearl Harbor*. The Admiral Nimitz Foundation, 1971.

O'Connor, Johnson. *English Vocabulary Builder* (Vol. II). Boston: Human Engineering Laboratory, 1974.

Officers' Christian Fellowship. *Christians and Military Service in Peace and War.* Englewood, CO: Officers' Christian Fellowship. Collection of essays.

Peel, William Carr and Walt Larimore. *Going Public With Your Faith: Becoming a Spiritual Influence at Work.* Read by William Carr Peel and Walt Larimore. Abridged. Grand Rapids, MI: Zondervan, 2003. Audiobook, 4 compact discs; 48 hours.

Phillips, Donald T. *Lincoln on Leadership: Executive Strategies for Tough Times.* New York: Warner Books, 1992.

Powell, Colin, and Klotz, Tony. *It Worked For Me in Life and Leadership.* New York, NY: Harper Collins, 2012.

Puryear, Jr., Edgar F. *19 Stars: A Study in Military Character and Leadership.* 2nd ed., 7th printing. Novato, CA: Presidio Press, 1988. First published 1971 by Green Publishers in Orange, VA.

"Quotes About Reality". *Goodreads.* Accessed 2012. http://www.good reads.com/quotes/tag/reality?auto_login_attempted=true.

"Quotes About Selflessness". *Goodreads.* Accessed 2012. http://www._goodreads.com/quotes/tag/selflessness.

Rath, Tom and Barry Conchie. *Strengths Based Leadership: Great Leaders, Teams, and Why People Follow.* New York: Gallup, 2008.

"Respectfully Quoted: A Dictionary of Quotations. 1989". *Bartleby.* 1993. Accessed June 2012. http://www.bartleby.com/73/1995.html

Roosevelt, Eleanor. *You Learn by Living: Eleven Keys for a More Fulfilling Life.* New York, NY: Harper Perennial/ Harper Collins, 1960.

Rose, P. F. "What Works: HALT — Hungry, Angry, Lonely, Tired". *Busted Halo.* August 10, 2009. Accessed December 2012. http://bustedhalo.com/features/what-works-10-halt-hungry-angry-lonely-tired

Sanders, J. Oswald. *Spiritual Leadership.* Chicago: Moody, 1967.

Scherkenbach, William W. *Deming's Road to Continual Improvement.* Knoxville, TN: SPC, 1991.

"Selfless Service Is Our Nation's Strength". *Reagan Quotes: Daily Quotes From the Statesman.* October 26, 2007. Accessed September 2012.
http://www.usma.edu/chaplain/SitePages/
Cadet%20Prayer.aspx

"Soldier Life". *U.S. Army — Army Strong.* Accessed August 20, 2012.
http://www.goarmy.com/soldier-life/being-a-soldier/living-the-army-values.noFlash.html

Starr, Kenneth. "A Legal View of Business Ethics." Lecture given at The Leader Board II Conference, Dallas Theological Seminary, Dallas, TX, May 3, 2004. Compact disc recording.

Sullivan, Gordon R. and Michael V. Harper. *Hope Is Not a Method: What Business Leaders Can Learn From America's Army.* New York: Times Business, 1996.

Sumner, Dr. Sarah. *Leadership above the Line.* Carol Stream, IL: Tyndale House, 2006.

Swenson, Richard A. *Margin: Restoring Emotional, Physical, Financial, and Time Reserves to Overloaded Lives.* Colorado Springs, CO: NavPress, 1992.

"The Gambler Lyrics". *Lyrics Freak.* 2013.
Accessed November 2012.
http://www.lyricsfreak.com/k/kenny+rogers/the+gambler_20077886.html

Thrall, Bill, Bruce McNicol, and Ken McElrath. *The Ascent of a Leader: How Ordinary Relationships Develop Extraordinary Character and Influence.* San Francisco: Jossey-Bass, 1999.

Tillman, Spencer. *Scoring in the Red Zone: How to Lead Successfully When the Pressure Is On.* Nashville, TN: Thomas Nelson, 2005.

Toogood, Granville N. *The Articulate Executive: Learn to Look, Act, and Sound Like a Leader.* New York: McGraw-Hill, 1996.

Townsend, John. *Leadership Beyond Reason: How Great Leaders Succeed by Harnessing the Power of Their Values, Feelings, and Intuition.* Nashville, TN: Thomas Nelson, 2009.

Viscount Slim. *Defeat Into Victory.* London, UK: Papermac, 1986. First published in hardback 1956 by Cassell & Company Limited.

Welch, Bobby. *You, The Warrior Leader: Applying Military Strategy for Victorious Spiritual Warfare.* Nashville, TN: Thomas Nelson, 2004.

Wheeler, Joe. *Abraham Lincoln: A Man of Faith and Courage.* New York: Howard Books, 2008.

Wooden, John. *They Call Me Coach.* With Jack Tobin. New York, NY: The McGraw-Hill Companies, 2004.

York, Daniel. *The Strong Leader's Hand*: *6 Essential Elements Every Leader Must Master.* Daniel York, 2011.

APPENDIX 1

Leader Self-Care Checkup and Tutorial

Adapted for applicability to leaders in all professions from:

COMPASSION FATIGUE: MANAGING YOURSELF

(Presented to DNA Military Chaplain's Retreat, October 6, 2012)

©2012 by Eric T. Scalise, Ph.D., LPC, LMFT

Leader Self-Care Checkup

INITIAL RESILIENT LEADER SELF-CARE CHECKUP QUESTION:

Three Primary Sources of Stress in my Ministry/Profession/Life are:

1. _____

_____

2. _____

_____

3. _____

_____

RELATED TO SOURCES OF STRESS IN MY LIFE:

1. Is my profession/ministry *CAUSING* the problems in my life?

_____

_____

2. Is my profession/ministry *REVEALING* the problems in my life?

_____

_____

RELATED TO THE BUILDING BLOCKS OF STRESS (fundamental life questions)

1. What am I supposed to be doing? ("Calling", use of personal gifts and skills, mission/purpose) (See Chapter 8, *Resilient Warriors*)

_____

_____

_____

2. Am I doing the right thing?

_____

_____

_____

3. Am I doing too much?

_____

_____

_____

4. Does what I do really matter?

_____

_____

_____

5. Am I isolated from supportive relationships?

_____

_____

_____

6. Do I seek to control which are actually beyond my control?

_____

_____

_____

<u>FINAL</u> RESILIENT LEADER SELF-CARE CHECKUP QUESTION:

Note: to be answered after reviewing Chapter 8, *Resilient Leaders*, and the leader self-care tutorial below.

My Personal Commitment:

Based on what God has been speaking to me regarding my own Comprehensive Self-Care™, I will **commit to change** by beginning with the following three things:

1. _____

_____

2. _____

_____

3. _____

_____

Leader Self-Care Tutorial

[NOTE: While useful as a "fill in the blank" exercise for class discussion, answers to self-care tutorial questions are *provided in all cap italics* in the text.]

A Look at "Your" Expectations

1. When you entered your ministry or profession, you probably expected to be *SUCCESSFUL*.

2. Leaders sometimes define success by *QUANTITATIVE* indicators as opposed to *QUALITATIVE* indicators such as those that make a difference in a person's life by helping them to become more Christ-like. (See Chapter 8 and 9,

Resilient Leaders, for examples from the life of Jesus.)

3. The discrepancy between ministerial or professional optimism and realism leads to *STRESS*.

A Look at "Their" Expectations

1. The *INDIVIDUAL* expectations may be legitimate. However, the *COMPOSITE* expectations can overwhelm you. (2 Corinthian 4:5 – "ourselves as your bondservants for Jesus' sake")

2. Leaders are often not allowed to hurt, fail, or be human.

3. People can sustain a false image of the leader as their hope for *A PERFECT PARENT*. This is the most common transference issue in ministry settings. People have the tendency to recreate their family of origin dynamics in other environments and relationships.

4. When you work harder on someone's personal responsibilities and wellbeing than they are, the individual has succeeded in giving you his/her job and you need to *SET BOUNDARIES*. (See story of the Rich Young Ruler (Matthew 19:16-24, Mark 10:17-25, Luke 18:18-25)

Responses to Unmet Expectations

When leaders realize they cannot live up to the overwhelming expectations, they may:

1. Develop a preoccupation with *STRESS PRODUCING* people or situations.

2. Over indulge in *ESCAPE BEHAVIORS* such as drugs, alcohol, sex, etc.

3. Avoid *INTIMACY* and seek *FANTASY* over reality.

4. Seek to *CONTROL* everything and everyone as a means to survive.

5. Justify their actions by *CRITICIZING* other things and other people.

6. Choose to simply *QUIT* their profession or the ministry.

The Neurobiology of Stress

- The brain has three primary parts: the hindbrain, the midbrain, and the forebrain.

- Forebrain includes the **cortex/neo-cortex** (cognition) and interacts with the **limbic system** (emotion).

- The feeling of pleasure is produced and regulated by a circuit of specialized nerve cells within the limbic system and is called the **nucleus accumbens**.

- The brain has 100 billion **neurons** (cells) – a strongly stimulated neuron can fire 1,000 times per second.

- The **amygdala** – plays a primary role in the processing and memory of emotional reactions.

- NEUROTRANSMITTERS: **chemical messengers** released by the electrical impulses of a neuron which record sensory experiences called **imprints**. These imprints are encoded, passed along appropriate pathways (across a **synapse**), and stored (usually at the unconscious level). Dopamine is one of the major agents related to the "**pleasure pathway**" to/through the limbic system. It plays a key role in love, sex and is instrumental in the development of addiction and stress responses.

- The primary stress hormones are ADRENALINE and CORTISOL.

- The *"fight"* or *"flight"* response is instinctive but often compromises RATIONAL or *CALM* thinking because adrenaline signals the body to move blood out of the brain and to the muscles where it may be needed more.

- The loss of pleasure and the rise of anhedronia: *anhedronia: an* (without or loss of) + *hedone* (pleasure or delight) = the **inability to derive pleasure out** of the ordinary things in life. Research has shown that ***multi-tasking, multi-processing***, and simultaneous ***multi-sensory inputting*** has a long-term destructive effect on the brain's pleasure system, as well as the ability to concentrate and focus. The result is what is referred to as ***dopamine flooding*** and ***hedonic dysregulation*** because the pleasure center is hijacked, alternative responses are not processed by the neo-cortex, and an addictive process is then created. Also described as ***emotional numbness, apathy, boredom***, and ***sadness*** (different than depression). Related to burnout, the very real consequence of ***over-stimulation,*** and *A MAJOR CAUSE OF MORAL FAILURE AMONG LEADERS.*

Other Consequences of Stress

- Dr. Hans Selye, a Canadian endocrinologist and the father of stress research, began to define stress in terms of the *"**General Adaptation Syndrome**"* during the 1950's.

He went on to define stress as the *"NON-SPECIFIC RESPONSE OF THE BODY TO ANY DEMAND."*

- Stress releases **adrenaline** and **cortisol** into the bloodstream with the potential for harmful effects over time:

1. a narrowing of the capillaries and other blood vessels leading in and out of the heart

2. a decrease in the flexibility and dilation properties of blood vessels and their endothelium linings

3. a decrease in the body's ability to flush excessive LDL cholesterol out of its system

4. a decrease of up to 50% in certain cognitive processes

5. an increase in the production of blood cholesterol (especially LDL)

6. an increase in the blood's tendency to clot

7. an increase in the depositing of plaque on the walls of the arteries

8. an increase in heart, breathing, and glycogen conversion rates

9. an increase for risk of cardiovascular disease, high blood pressure, stroke, and a compromise of the body's immune system

- According to the American Institute on Stress, **80-90%** of all doctor's visits are stress-related.

- According to the American Heart Association, more than **50 million** Americans suffer from high blood pressure and nearly **60 million** suffer from some form of cardiovascular disease, resulting in over 1 million deaths each year (2 out of every five that die or 1 every 32 seconds).

- Heart disease has been the **leading cause of death** in the United States every year since 1900 (except 1918) and crosses all racial, gender, socioeconomic, and age barriers.

- According to the U.S. Dept. of Health and Human Services, **25%** of all prescriptions written in the United States are for tranquilizers, antidepressants, and anti-anxiety medication.

- **Compassion** comes from the Latin word, **compat**, which means "to suffer with." It has been defined as: "feelings of deep sympathy or sorrow for another who is stricken by sufferings or misfortune, accompanied by a strong desire to alleviate pain or remove its cause." **Compassion Fatigue** refers to emotional, physical, and spiritual exhaustion that gradually impacts a person's capacity to experience joy, or to feel and care for others. It is sometimes referred to as *SECONDARY* or *VICARIOUS* traumatic stress and is associated with the "HIGH COST OF CARING". The effects of stress and compassion fatigue, like sleep-loss, are *ACCUMULATIVE.*

- **Useful websites:**

  www.compassionfatigue.org/index.html

  www.proqol.org/ProQol_Test.html

  www.figleyinstitute.com/indexMain.html

  www.scholar.google.com/scholar?q=compassion+fatigue+figley&hl=en&as_sdt=0&as_vis=1&oi=scholart

- **Useful Bible Verses** related to the physiological impacts of stress:

  1. "<u>Anxiety in a man's heart</u> weighs it down (literally), but a good word makes it glad." (Proverbs 12:25, underline and parenthetical comment added)

  2. "<u>Put on a heart</u> of compassion, kindness, humility, gentleness, and patience." (Colossians 3:12b, underline added)

The Two Categories of Stress

1. First, there is the stress of *ONE'S PROFESSION/MINISTRY*.

2. Second, there is the stress *I BRING INTO PROFESSION/MINISTRY*.

Leaders who have dealt with the *SECOND* category of stress, can better handle the *FIRST* category of stress. Ask yourself, or ask someone close to you:

1. Is my profession/ministry *CAUSING* the problems in my life? _____ ,*or*

2. Is my profession/ministry *REVEALING* the problems in my life? _____

Leading Yourself

1. Don't forget your *FIRST LOVE* because *YOU* are not your profession/ministry.

   "And He appointed twelve, so that they would be with Him and that He could send them out to preach and to have authority to cast out demons." (Mark 3:14-15)

   "...and you have perseverance and have endured for My name's sake, and have not grown weary. But I have this against you, that you have left your first love."
   (Revelation 2:3-4)

2. Learn what it means to have *JOY* and understand that it is not the same thing as *HAPPINESS* or *PLEASURE*.

   "But realize this, that in the last days difficult times will come. For men will be lovers of self, lovers of money, boastful, arrogant, revilers, disobedient to parents, ungrateful, unholy, unloving, irreconcilable, malicious gossips, without self-control, brutal, haters of good, treacherous, reckless, conceited, **lovers of pleasure** rather than lovers of God, holding to a form of godliness, though they have denied its power." (2 Timothy 3:1-5, italics and bold emphasis added)

"You will make known to me the path of life; in Your presence is fullness of joy; in Your right hand there are pleasures forever." (Psalm 16:11)

"Create in me a clean heart, O God, and renew a steadfast spirit within me. Do not cast me away from Your presence and do not take Your Holy Spirit from me. Restore to me the joy of Your salvation and sustain me with a willing spirit. Then I will teach transgressors Your ways and sinners will be converted to You." (Psalm 51:10-13)

3. Learn to *DEPERSONALIZE* the process and limit your time around *NEGATIVE PEOPLE*.

"Finally brethren, whatever is true, whatever is honorable, whatever is right, whatever is pure, whatever is lovely, whatever is of good repute, if there is excellence and if anything worthy of praise, **dwell on these things**." (Philippians 4:8, italics and bold emphasis added)

4. Learn to *REST* because God has a lot to say about *REST*, and slow down the *RATE OF CHANGE*.

"Therefore, let us fear if, while a promise remains of **entering His rest**, any one of you may have come short of it... For we who have believed **enter that rest**... So there remains a **Sabbath rest** for the people of God. For the one who has **entered His rest** has himself also **rested** from his works, as God did from His." (Hebrews 4:1-10, italics and bold emphasis added)

"Though youths grow weary and tired, and vigorous young men stumble badly, yet those who wait for the Lord will gain new strength. They will mount up with wings like eagles; they will run and not get tired; they will walk and not become weary." (Isaiah 40:30-31)

"If the axe is dull and he does not **sharpen** its edge, then he must exert more strength." (Ecclesiastes 10:10, bold emphasis added)

5. Maintain a healthy foundation of *SLEEP* in your daily routine.

"In peace I will both lie down and **sleep**, for You alone, O Lord, make me to dwell in safety." (Psalm 4:8, bold emphasis added)

"When you lie down, you will not be afraid; when you lie down, your **sleep** will be sweet." (Proverbs 3:24, bold emphasis added)

6. Pay attention to *DIET* and *EXERCISE* regimens.

"All things are lawful for me, but **not all things are profitable**. All things are lawful for me, but I will not be mastered by anything. Food is for the stomach and the stomach is for food, but God will do away with both of them, yet **the body is not for immorality**, but for the Lord, and **the Lord is for the body**. Now God has not only raised the Lord, but will also raise us up through His power. Do you know that **your bodies are members of Christ**? (1 Corinthians 6:12-15, italics and bold emphasis added)

"Do you not know that **your body is a temple** of the Holy Spirit who is in you, whom you have from God, and that you are not your own? For you have been bought with a price: therefore **glorify God in your body**."
(1 Corinthians 6:19-20, italics and bold emphasis added)

7. Learn to be *SILENT* and learn to be *STILL*.

"But Jesus Himself would **often slip away** to the wilderness and pray." (Luke 5:16, italics and bold emphasis added)

"**Be still** and know that I am God." (Psalm 46:10, italics and bold emphasis added)

"But know that the Lord has set apart the godly man for Himself; the Lord hears when I call Him. Tremble, and do not sin; meditate in your heart upon your bed, and **be still**." (Psalm 43:3-4, italics and bold emphasis added)

"The Lord is good to those who wait for Him, to the person who seeks Him. It is good that he **waits silently** for the salvation of the Lord." (Lamentations 3:25-26, italics and bold emphasis added)

8. Create *OUTLETS* to avoid stagnation.

   "**Give**, and it shall be given to you. They will pour it into your lap a good measure, pressed down, shaken together, and running over. For by your standard of measure it will be measured to you in return." (Luke 6:38, italics and bold emphasis added)

   "If anyone is thirsty, let him come to Me and drink. He who believes in Me, as the Scripture said, 'From his innermost being will flow rivers of **living water**." (John 7:37-38, italics and bold emphasis added)

9. Seek to give your *BURDENS* to God each day.

   "Cast your **burden** upon the Lord and He will sustain you; He will never allow the righteous to be shaken." (Psalm 55:22, italics and bold emphasis added)

   "Blessed be the Lord, who daily bears our **burden**, the God who is our salvation." (Psalm 68:10, italics and bold emphasis added)

   "Come to Me, all you who are **weary and heavy laden**, and I will give you rest. Take My yoke upon you and learn from Me, for I am gentle and humble in heart, and you will find rest for your souls. For **My yoke is easy** and My burden is light." (Matthew 11:28-30, italics and bold emphasis added)

10. Learn to *TRIAGE* your daily and your life events.

"Teach me good **discernment** and knowledge, for I believe in Your commandments." (Psalm 119:66, italics and bold emphasis added)

"The **steps** of a man are established by the Lord and He delights in his way." (Psalm 37:23, italics and bold emphasis added)

11. Learn to have realistic *EXPECTATIONS* of yourself and others.

"**Discretion** will guard you, **understanding** will watch over you." (Proverbs 2:11, italics and bold emphasis added)

"For He Himself knows **our frame**; He is mindful that we are but dust." (Psalm 103:14, italics and bold emphasis added)

12. *RESOLVE* those things that can be attended to easily and quickly.

"Catch the foxes for us, the **little foxes** that are ruining the vineyards while our vineyards are in blossom."
(Song of Solomon 2:15, italics and bold emphasis added)

"A **little leaven** leavens the whole lump of dough." (Galatians 5:9, italics and bold emphasis added)

13. Learn to *MANAGE* your time by saying "*NO*," or your time will control you.

"There is an **appointed time** for everything. And there is a **time** for every event under heaven... He has made everything appropriate in its **time**." (Ecclesiastes 3:1-11, italics and bold emphasis added)

"But as for me, I trust in You, O Lord, I say, 'You are my God.' **My times** are in Your hands." (Psalm 31:14-15, italics and bold emphasis added)

14. Learn to *DELEGATE* to others whenever, wherever, and however it is appropriate.

Jethro counsels Moses: "The thing that you are doing is not good. **You will surely wear out**, both yourself and these people who are with you, for the task is too heavy for you; **you cannot do it alone**." (Exodus 18:13-26, italics and bold emphasis added)

The Apostles respond to the need: "Therefore, brethren, select among you seven men of good reputation, full of the Spirit and of wisdom, **whom we may put in charge of this task**." (Acts 6:1-5, italics and bold emphasis added)

"The things which you have heard from me in the presence of many witnesses, **entrust these** to faithful men who will be able to teach others also." (2 Timothy 2:2, italics and bold emphasis added)

15. Find one or two key people in your life to be *ACCOUNTABLE* to.

"Be of sober spirit, be on the alert. Your adversary, the devil, prowls around like a roaring lion, *seeking someone to devour.*" (1 Peter 5:8, italics and bold emphasis added)

Isolation is the enemy's plan: "Simon, Simon, behold, Satan has demanded permission to *sift you like wheat*; but I have prayed for you that your faith may not fail." (Luke 22:31-32, italics and bold emphasis added)

Who is standing with you? (1 Kings 4:1-6)

<u>FINAL</u> RESILIENT LEADER SELF-CARE CHECKUP QUESTION:

Note: to be answered after reviewing Chapter 8, *Resilient Leaders*, and the leader self-care tutorial above.

My Personal Commitment:

Based on what God has been speaking to me regarding my own Comprehensive Self-Care™, I will *commit to change* by beginning with the following three things:

1. _____

_____

2. _____

   _____

3. _____

   _____

Additional Leader Self-Care Notes:

_____

_____

_____

_____

_____

_____

_____

_____

_____

_____

_____

_____

_____

_____

_____

_____

_____

_____

_____

_____

_____

With special appreciation to Dr. Eric Scalise for permission to use
this helpful self-care tutorial.

APPENDIX 2

Consolidated Resilient Leader Takeaways

Chapter 1 – Leadership: A Contact Sport

RL 1 – Leadership is a contact sport. Expect tribulation.

RL 2 – In the rough and tumble of life, leadership makes a difference. Excellent leadership (to which we aspire) integrates disciplines which ensure personal resilience, and promote resilience in others and in organizations.

RL 3 – Resilient Leadership is Selfless Service over time from a platform of character and competence.

RL 4 – An essential ingredient of Resilient Leadership is leading with excellence *over time* through the realities of success and failure in the tough marketplaces of life.

RL 5 – Great, resilient leaders make a positive difference in the lives of others, and they do it consistently.

RL 6 – Good or great leadership is always preferred, but tragic accidents and circumstances frequently happen under the supervision of good leaders doing the right thing for the right reasons.

RL 7 – Crisis defines the character of the Leader.

RL 8 – Hurting people often strike out at the nearest target or symbol of authority. Leaders must understand this and recognize the need to be a "heat shield" that graciously and securely absorbs the fiery darts from angry and disillusioned people and protects the organization and others from undue distraction to the mission.

RL 9 – Leaders must use crises as "teachable moments" for themselves and others which accelerate learning, trust, and systemic improvements.

RL 10 – Assumption of command is a clear defining moment when the challenge and privilege of command is transitioned into new hands. A proper "succession of leadership" means the newly appointed leader is in charge, and the former leader departs the scene, giving wide latitude to the new leader as he engages with his subordinate team, shapes new policies, and integrates his own personality and experience into the life of the organization.

RL 11 – Leaders with "Authority" to fulfill "Responsibility" are subject to "Accountability."

RL 12 – Risk management is a critical leader competency for leaders at all levels in all professions. While great leaders can't always prevent bad outcomes, it is critical that every leader develop a sixth sense regarding risk to the operation and the personnel which he oversees.

Chapter 2 – Character Counts I: Selfless Service

RL 13 – While competencies are important, character is the trump card.

RL 14 – Selfless Service, Integrity, and Courage form a three strand cord of Character that is not easily broken.

RL 15 – Selfless Service is "serving others without regard for self" and inherently includes personal sacrifice.

RL 16 – Resilience in leadership means leading with excellence *over time* through the realities of success and failure in the tough marketplaces of life.

RL 17 – The proper motives of the leader directly spring from a spirit of Selfless Service.

RL 18 – Maybe you can also identify with this progression from mental assent, to heartfelt compassion, to divine calling to serve others at the expense of self.... Or maybe you are not there yet.

Chapter 3 – Character Counts II: Integrity and Courage

RL 19 – Not telling a lie is fundamental, but this is only the beginning of integrity.

RL 20 – Integrity on a higher plane is the seamless integration of faith, family, and profession into a God-honoring life message.

RL 21 – Our lives need full integration across the broad range of faith, family, and profession, but when a threat does arise, integrity also requires that we quickly identify the problem, seal off the broader impacts, and address the personal or corporate issue.

RL 22 – FAITH is the bridge which leads from FEAR to COURAGE, helping us to "hold on ten seconds longer."

RL 23 – Courage grows each time we stare down fear.

RL 24 – Courage is the cumulative result of staring down fear across the full spectrum of the physical, mental, spiritual, emotional, and relational domains.

RL 25 – Courage must be balanced with selflessness and integrity.

Chapter 4 – Wisdom: The Bridge Between Character and Competence

RL 26 – WISDOM is necessary to balance other highly commendable qualities of character. For example, without wisdom, courage can easily turn to folly.

RL 27 – May we not pursue the fleeting trappings of leadership, but may we pursue wisdom and knowledge for the benefit of those we lead.

RL 28 – Wisdom positively influences the leader's decision making, growth, investment in others, awareness of inadequacy and vulnerability, sense of timing, clarity regarding sources of strength, ability to craft vision, and discernment regarding pace and capacity.

RL 29 – Wise leaders must exercise integrity to take full responsibility for the outcome of their decisions.

RL 30 – Wise leaders learn and grow for a lifetime.

RL 31 – Wise leaders mentor others, having a profound impact upon the personal and professional future of a willing learner.

RL 32 – The Bible is a storehouse of wisdom.

Chapter 5 – Voice in the Dark!—Leading Before Crisis

RL 33 – "Condition Setting," applicable across all arenas of life and leadership, is the leader's responsibility to do everything possible before a complex or dangerous mission to ensure successful accomplishment at a minimum of risk to personnel and other resources.

RL 34 – "Do your soldiers know your voice in the dark?" refers to setting the conditions of trust and confidence between leader and led.

RL 35 – "Do you know your troops?" is a condition setter which emphasizes the leader's appreciation of the unique strengths, weaknesses, and personal bent of those they lead.

RL 36 – Simplicity is a leader virtue, allowing communication of profound and difficult concepts which ensures necessary understanding and application.

RL 37 – Four essential leadership fundamentals are Vision, Team, Reality, and Growth.

RL 38 – VISION is a clear <u>focus</u> upon a future <u>end state</u> that <u>propels self and others forward with expectation and perseverance</u>.

RL 39 – Vision is essential, but not sufficient without practical strategies to operationalize the vision. Strategic planning is an essential supporting competency. The leader must guide his team in operationalizing the vision by implementing supportive strategies and intermediate objectives which move the team successfully toward the desired future.

RL 40 – TEAM is a group of <u>interdependent</u> players who exercise <u>uniquely valuable functions</u> towards the <u>accomplishment</u> of a <u>shared vision and mission</u>.

RL 41 – The leader is responsible for guiding his team in defining the desired future end state, and to articulate it to his team clearly, confidently, and consistently.

RL 42 – The team that "owns the vision" can better maintain momentum in order to achieve it. The wise visionary leader will often slow down to allow the team to discover the vision themselves and embrace it at an early stage in the process.

RL 43 – REALITY is important for leaders who need facts, not fiction. It is important for leaders to value reality as a friend. Leaders who avoid bad news are condemning themselves to a fantasy world where failure to deal with reality only defers and magnifies the eventual consequences.

RL 44 – GROWTH is an essential organizational goal that prevents stagnation, leads to new opportunities and approaches, and instills a quest for continuous improvement.

Chapter 6 – Sir, We Have A Situation!—Leading During Crisis

RL 45 – Crisis Leaders honor the dead and lead the living.

RL 46 – Crisis Leaders positively affirm those in the crucible of crisis. They give life to confused, scared, and disconsolate followers.

RL 47 – Crisis Leaders know when to stay out of the way, letting experts do their job in time sensitive settings of urgency.

RL 48 – Crisis Leaders seek historical parallels. Someone has been here before! How did they handle it?

RL 49 – Crisis Leaders shield their subordinates from outside distractors, helping them focus on the crisis at hand.

RL 50 – Crisis Leaders lead by example, taking action when paralysis and fear have immobilized others.

RL 51 – Crisis Leaders mobilize external resources for the good of the cause, using their authority and influence to truly help their subordinates resolve the crisis.

RL 52 – Biblical and contemporary role models provide unlimited instruction and inspiration regarding crisis leadership. We should study them well.

Chapter 7 – I'd Rather Hide!—Leading After Crisis

RL 53 – <u>Many times leaders want to hide</u> during the most challenging "bounce back" phase, rather than facing the tough tasks of grieving, rebuilding, regaining momentum, and renewing hope. Resilient leaders are the ones who can and must guide their team through this season of restoration and growth.

RL 54 – In <u>rebuilding the team</u> after a seismic shock has rocked the organization, the resilient leader needs to seize the opportunity to revalidate that his players are in the optimal role for them and for the team, ensuring best alignment of personnel resources with the necessary functions of the organization.

RL 55 – In the rough and tumble world of business, parenting, teaching others, care giving, and most certainly military leadership with complex training scenarios and unpredictable battlefields, failure is a very possible outcome even for the very best of leaders. Resilient leaders must <u>underwrite mistakes</u> as a key means to growing future leaders.

RL 56 – While it is important for an outfit to quickly move past tragedy and trauma, it is also naive for a leader to not understand that grieving and healing take time. When the dense fog of pain and suffering lies heavy upon troops and their families, resilient leaders must <u>mourn with those who mourn</u>.

RL 57 – A resilient leader who is a <u>merchant of hope</u> does not deny present suffering for himself and others, yet he conveys optimism, helping others hold on for a better tomorrow.

RL 58 – Organizational bounce back includes <u>revalidating the azimuth</u> to ensure that energy applied to recovery is well focused and pointed in the right direction. This includes developing a <u>keen appreciation of current and future market conditions</u> as well as <u>developing a proactive battle rhythm</u> which helps to foresee and shape the future.

RL 59 – <u>Do your troops know that you need them</u>? is a condition setter which emphasizes team. Resilient leaders empower others, particularly when they are helping their organization bounce back, when they are breathing new life into followers and teams who have experienced challenging times.

RL 60 – The ethic of <u>learning</u> from life experiences and <u>adapting</u> to meet future demands lies at the heart of resilient life and leadership.

Chapter 8 – "Careful Your Well of Courage!"—Leader Self-Care

RL 61 – The reality is that we all have a reservoir, a well of courage, which is limited in capacity and must be refilled to avoid depletion.

RL 62 – "How do we not grow weary and lose heart as leaders?" is one of the most relevant questions of our time and critical to the subject of resilient leadership. Resilient leaders know how to counteract continual stressors in order to stay in the game.

RL 63 – To help others we must first help ourselves.

RL 64 – The leader competency to offset excessive stress and burnout is "Comprehensive Self-Care™" aimed at continual renewal across the full spectrum of physical, mental, spiritual, emotional, and relational fitness.

RL 65 – While longer periods of rest are important, daily and weekly "disciplines of replenishment" are the real antidote to stressful living and potential burnout.

RL 66 – Sabbath Rest, Work Ending Rituals, Lowering Ambient Noise, Visualization, Spiritual Meditation, and Sleep Management are important techniques of replenishment.

RL 67 – Recent findings regarding brain chemistry reinforce the importance of sleep management to minimize the psychological and physiological impacts of sleep loss.

RL 68 – Personal Risk Management™ is a critical leader skill. "HALT" is a useful acronym to alert leaders to particular vulnerability when they are Hungry, Angry, Lonely, or Tired.

Chapter 9 – Follow Me!—The Ultimate Resilient Leader

RL 69 – Jesus led by example, from the front, not asking His followers to do anything He would not do.

RL 70 – Throughout His life as a leader, Jesus practiced what today we would call "leader development," consistently investing in the growth of others.

RL 71 – Leadership is highly relational and ultimately about sacrificial love between leader and led.

RL 72 – As modeled by Jesus, a leader must draw others back to the high and noble calling for which they serve.

RL 73 – Leaders must continue to follow the prime example of Jesus and other leadership role models without getting derailed by other things.

RL 74 – Whether you think Jesus was merely a great person and prophet, or you are a true follower of Christ; one cannot address the full spectrum of leadership without paying close attention to the person of Jesus, along with the spiritual wellbeing of those they lead.

RL 75 – The Bible is the world's greatest leadership manual.

RL 76 – Jesus was the Ultimate Resilient Leader. Focus on Him. Consider Him. Follow Him.

APPENDIX 3

Resilient Nations

Introduction

"The people don't have a will to work" stated the Bulgarian President after I queried, "What is your biggest problem?" While I will address this interaction at greater length in *Resilient Nations*, this answer was very telling. While the President could have identified the need for tangible resources (money, natural resources, trading partners, industrial production, and others), he instead identified a very intangible, internal attribute he termed "will to work." Where does that come from? How does a nation lose such essential qualities? How do they get them back?

The reality is that nations have many different "infrastructures" which are critical to their survival and success as a nation state. Some of these infrastructures may immediately come to mind: banking, politics, national security, energy, commerce, and others. While all of these are very important, a nation's intangible moral-spiritual infrastructure undergirds all these other elements of national power and existence. This moral-spiritual infrastructure (MSI) includes critical arenas such as the strength of its families, the ethics of its boardrooms, the civility of its discourse, adherence to the rule of law, respect for lives of the unborn and the elderly, regard for the security of future generations, the education of our youth, the relevance of our faith communities, the adherence to national values and accurate historical roots, and the resilience and enterprise of our citizens—including their "will to work." All of these intangible elements of MSI are essential to a nation's identity and survival as an entity which is truly a benefit to its citizens and the world community.

Resilient Nations will explore such issues, first in a generic sense from a conceptual perspective, and then very specifically applied to the United States of America. What is our current "State of the Union?" What is the status of our MSI at the beginning of the 21st Century? Is our MSI solid and stable, or is it sadly weakened, on the brink of collapse and irreversible consequence? Are life, liberty, and the pursuit of happiness still relevant and reachable? Will our MSI, which provided a bedrock foundation from the first days of this Republic (and through subsequent wars, depressions, and national calamities) allow for the continuation of our "American way of life?" Or is that a thing of the past?

Resilient Nations is the last component of *The Resilience Trilogy*. In *Resilient Warriors* we addressed individual resilience, recognizing that we are all warriors on the playing fields of every marketplace and endeavor. How high do we bounce when we are body-slammed to the hard concrete of life? How do we build such bounce ahead of time? How do we weather the storm? After trials and tribulations, how do we bounce back without getting stuck in toxic emotions of guilt, false guilt, anger, bitterness? Then how do we "learn & adapt" for the inevitable next life challenge? We cited many role models of resilience, most particularly the Ultimate Resilient Warrior, Jesus.

In *Resilient Leaders*, we applied these same concepts to the leader level. How do leaders prepare themselves, their organizations, and those they lead to also be resilient? How does a leader "selflessly serve over time from a platform of character and competence?" We looked at key attributes such as selflessness, integrity, courage, and wisdom. Then we applied the Resilience Life Cycle© directly to leadership: How does a leader "set the conditions" (before) for the success of his organization and his followers? What does an "in extremis leader" (during) look like, helping other navigate crisis? How does a leader then move others into a new and hopeful future, cultivating a learning organization which "talks to itself?" In like manner, we also considered many leader role models and related numerous personal stories, recognizing again that Jesus is the Ultimate Resilient Leader and the Bible is the world's greatest leadership manual. We can do no better than to "lead like Jesus."

Now we consider resilience applied to Nations. The ultimate question: can the United States of America strengthen its MSI in the 21st Century, bouncing back from decades of moral erosion, spiritual skepticism, and alarming trend lines which counter the proposition that we are "the greatest nation on Earth?" Can we weather the current storms which threaten national survival? Can we bounce back to our former greatness, America? Are we still a Resilient Nation?

In Gibbon's *Decline and Fall of the Roman Empire,* the Roman Senators' wives became prostitutes on the temple mount. At the height of Roman decadence, good became evil and evil became good. One can rightly argue that the United States is frightfully close to a similar fate.

Prayerfully, it is not too late.

Prayerfully, we can demonstrate the resilience and rightness that have characterized America for the last 237 years.

Prayerfully, *Resilient Nations*, along with other like-minded harbingers, will help turn the tide.

Prayerfully, the United States will mount a moral and spiritual rearmament that is as transformational as were the First and Second Great Awakenings in this nation's history.

Prayerfully, God will not give up on us yet.

Prayerfully, the best for America is yet to come. Only time will tell.

Only concerned and committed Americans can make the difference.

Let us begin.

APPENDIX 4

Products and Services

FOR SUPPORTING RESILIENCE CONTENT
www.ResilienceTrilogy.com

FOR SPECIFIC BOOK INFORMATION & ORDERING
RESILIENT WARRIORS
www.ResilientWarriorsBook.com
ISBN: 978-0-9838919-4-9

RESILIENT WARRIORS ADVANCED STUDY GUIDE
www.ResilientWarriorsBook.com
ISBN: 978-0-9838919-5-6

RESILIENT LEADERS
www.ResilientLeadersBook.com
ISBN: 978-0-9855979-9-3

RESILIENT NATIONS **(Summer 2014)**
www.ResilientNationsBook.com

FOR INFORMATION, COMMENTS, and QUESTIONS
author@resiliencetrilogy.com
administrator@resiliencetrilogy.com

RFD LLC, P.O. Box 5336, Williamsburg, VA 23188

Index

CPSIA information can be obtained
at www.ICGtesting.com
Printed in the USA
BVOW09s0724060418

512651BV00002B/181/P